SURVIVING TERRORISM

SURVIVING TERRORISM

HOW TO UNDERSTAND, ANTICIPATE, AND RESPOND TO TERRORIST ATTACKS

RAINER STAHLBERG

Fort Lee, New Jersey

Published by Barricade Books Inc.
185 Bridge Plaza North
Suite 308-A
Fort Lee, NJ 07024
www.barricadebooks.com

Library of Congress Cataloging-in-Publication Data

Stahlberg, Rainer.
        Surviving Terrorism : how to understand, anticipate, and respond to ter-
rorist attacks / Rainer Stahlberg.
        p. cm.
Includes bibliographical references.
ISBN 1-56980-230-0 (pbk. : alk. paper)
1. Terrorism. 2. Survival skills. 3. Survival after airplane accidents, shipwrecks, etc. I.
Title.

HV6431 .S698 2002
613.6--dc21

2002016398

Manufactured in the United States of America
First Printing

SURVIVING TERRORISM

CONTENTS

INTRODUCTION

We thought we were invincible. We thought we were impenetrable. We were so confident. We were the premier power on earth, and we were a bit arrogant about it. We were so sure, then a ragtag bunch kicked us right in the privates to remind us of our vulnerability.

Talking to a friend from Jersey City brought home the impact the September 11 attacks had on us all. He related that being across from New York City and seeing fighter planes patrolling the airspace, he realized how vulnerable we are. Practically all of us felt shell-shocked when we saw what happened in New York, Washington, and in the Pennsylvania countryside.

Most commentators say that on September 11, the world changed. On that date, much like when Pearl Harbor was attacked, it was brought home to us that we were asleep at the switch. We had been lulled into a false sense of security. We thought, "It won't happen here." But with those who argue that the world changed, I beg to differ. On September 11, we had a greater portion of the geopolitical landscape revealed to us. On September 11, we realized that while we were consumed with the tabloid liaisons of our leaders, we had a covert war declared against our Western ideals.

INTRODUCTION

A close examination of recent history reveals all of the indicators of the September 11 attacks. The use of airplanes as missiles is not exactly new. Back in the early 1990s, a demented passenger shot the pilot, and the plane went down. A disgruntled FedEx flight engineer attempted to take over its plane with the express purpose of crashing it into the FedEx head-quarters. More recently, a light plane attempted to crash into the White House. The method used was not exactly novel, and the seeds of hatred of the West had long been sown. Now that the Iraqi regime has been over-thrown we may see an escalation of terrorist attacks in the U.S.A.

• • •

The terrorists will go after soft targets: civilians. They want to kill and maim as many of us as they can in the name of religion.

The first war of the new millennium is a religious war in the eyes of the aggressors. Our enemies in this war are a group of people using twenty-first century equipment to force the world to return to the eighth-century mores of the Islamic world.

Keep in mind that extreme Islamists are not the only ones with a grudge against America. There are other groups with the desire, the money, and the equipment out there to hurt us. The only difference is that al-Qaeda planned ahead and was the first off the mark. The copycats are coming in the second wave.

This current wave of terrorism represents a change in the behavior of terrorists. We were used to plane hijackings whereby keeping our cool and supplying pizza to the perpetrators eventually lead to the release of the plane and passengers. In the past terrorists demanded liberation of this or that piece of real estate and their colleagues in custody. Today there are no demands, no communication, just maximum use of the people and the tools on hand to cause maximum loss of life. This shift of paradigm by necessity forces us to rethink our methods of defense. For instance, hostages must now resist terrorists even if it results in their own loss of life. Today hostages know that their lives are forfeit in any case. It is my purpose to examine current circumstances and provide a blueprint for survival in the current climate of global terrorism.

The terrorists will go after soft targets: civilians. They want to kill and maim as many of us as they can in the name of religion. We heard that they boasted that they would fight to the death in Afghanistan. We obliged them. The same pattern repeats itself in Israel. When soundly beaten, they want to reason with us. Would the president sit down with Osama bin Laden to discuss peace? Hell no.

What the terrorists want to do is rob us of the fruits of our civilization. Our advances in medicine and technology are offensive to them. No matter what practitioners of psychobabble say, I suspect that they hate us because deep down they realize that they are unable to compete in our world. Another goal is to deny our freedoms by turning our country into a police state closely resembling the mullah-infested world of theirs. It is my goal to provide readers with the survival skills to prevent terrorists' victory.

In the fight against these groups, the biggest mistake we can make is to generalize or, as currently called, profile people of the nations or religious groups who are identified with these atrocities. Most of the Muslim people living in this country are here for precisely the same reason our ancestors immigrated here, to escape oppressive governments. To label them does injustice to our history and deprives us an extremely important intelligence asset. Surviving terrorism requires more intelligence than "Islamophobia," which, unfortunately, is on the rise out on the streets of the nation.

• • •

Rather than discussing the evolution of terrorist organizations, I will try to focus on what terrorists are capable of and what practical steps you, as an individual, can take to protect yourself against them. The resources available to the government are not within reach of the average citizen, so we must make do with what is available to us. Fortunately much of the military equipment used has civilian counterparts, making our task somewhat easier.

Many survival books stress the need for relocating to small towns or having retreats. Being a realist, I won't do this. More than 80 percent of Americans live in urban environments because that is where the jobs are. I'll focus instead on what to do in densely populated areas. The counter-terrorism experts are up sleepless at night worrying about bioterrorism. They are not worried about anthrax. Anthrax is a "one on one" weapon (each person has to be individually infected). The experts are worried about diseases like smallpox, the "gift that keeps on giving." You can draw a concentric circle around the first victim, and it radiates out spreading easily with up to a 60-percent fatality rate.

American experts are looking at between seventy and one hundred high impact sites in America. Our allies in Britain, Canada, and Australia have far fewer potential targets. (Note that these are all English-speaking countries.) At this point, the international terrorists are focusing on these countries and Israel. Today's terrorists will use our own public services, transportation methods, and even government systems to strike at us. Given that fact, it would take a thirty-volume encyclopedia to catalog all possible attacks. In this book, I will focus on the most likely scenarios and the ones that you can most effectively defend against.

Because of the forceful international response and subsequent aid provided to the Northern and Eastern Alliance, Afghanistan has a chance to recover from a twenty-three-year-old war. How will this play out? Time will tell. The actions against the Taliban put other terrorist organizations on notice that the American government can project power even to the most remote corner of the world. A combination of aircraft carriers, long-range bombers, helicopter assault ships, and ground forces will make any nation sponsoring or basing terrorist organizations think long and hard about their actions.

Despite this, the reality is that we will be on the target list for terrorist organizations as long as Western countries are viewed as willing to export capital to Third World countries to take advantage of cheap labor and poor environmental practices. As long as they think that we close our borders to legitimate immigrants and enact protectionist import regulations, we will fan the fuels of rage against us. We have to take a good look in the mirror and change if we must. We have to do a better job showing the totality of our way of life. But right now, we must prepare ourselves against terrorist strikes to defend our way of life.

1
PRE-SEPTEMBER 11 VIEW OF THE WORLD THROUGH ROSE-COLORED GLASSES

"The future is made of the same stuff as the present."
—Simone Weil

Pre-September 11 trends show that the world in the twenty-first century will be more crowded, more polluted, poorer, more stressed, and more prone to violence. The cost of food, energy, transportation, services, and other items will rise while the majority will earn less. The desperately poor will continue to starve. More than 90 percent of the population growth is expected to be in cities. As it is, urban infrastructures don't adequately support the people who live there. Life for billions is precarious now.

These trends provided a fertile recruiting ground for terrorists with a grudge. The leaders come from middle- or even upper-class backgrounds and are, for the most part, highly educated. As an astute historian observed, revolutions break out not when the situation is at its bleakest, but when things improve. Using this as a guide, there may be as many of five major revolutions in the near future. As usual, the U.S. will be blamed for what has befallen the people.

The countries that host terrorist groups are still in an agricultural economy, or what Alvin Toffler calls a First Wave economy. Land and farm labor are their main means of production. Indonesia, Pakistan, and other developing Muslim nations are in a Second Wave economy. Their land remains valuable while labor becomes centralized around machines and larger industries. As nations industrialize, people move from farms and villages to the cities, leaving fewer laborers to produce food. Mechanized farming solves this problem.

Looking through rose-colored glasses, we envisioned a steady progress to industrialization, improved working conditions, and a fairer distribution of the fruits of progress. Removing these glasses, we see twenty countries producing almost 90 percent of the wealth and in developing countries two classes of people, the super rich and the super poor. Much like it was some five hundred years ago. This adds to the real and imagined woes fueling the rage that leads to terrorism.

The end of the Cold War caused a major change in the geopolitical landscape. Whatever you think of the Cold War, everyone knows it was a time in which the old conservative strictures against big government were put on hold. Both the friends and enemies of a huge standing military knew it was impossible to maintain a commitment to a constitutional republic while trying to defeat an enemy halfway around the globe and destabilizing any government not following State Department orders.

Indeed, the Cold War cemented national loyalties, undermined localism and individualism, and suppressed opposition to government policy, forging a culture of fear and statism. The Cold War portrayed the central state as the only thing standing between nuclear annihilation and us. If conservatives had to put up with the liberal welfare and regulatory state for the sake of national survival, so be it. The legacy of the Cold War was the formation of new countries and the creation of more terrorist groups than we can count.

Global instability rose from the ashes of the Cold War. This new instability gave rise to increased smuggling, slave labor, arms trade, and, of course, the bases for training terrorists. Some countries, like Somalia, have no central government, and warlords control areas where they are a law unto themselves. Other countries are pawns in a regional game for acquiring their resources. These resources then find their way into terrorist hands. There are more U.S. $100 bills circulating around the world than in the U.S.

Money is required to finance terrorist activities. True, there is a definite trend toward direct deposits of government payments and payroll earnings. Yet at the same time we see more and more government intrusion into the financial activities people undertake. For example, depending on where you live, the banks have to report any large cash deposits (as low as $3,000). Given the rise of the underground economy, many opt to deal in cash and opt out of the normal banking system. So the cashless direction has an equally strong counterdirection built in, which favors cash transactions only. A confusing state of affairs and the final outcome is far from clear.

In many countries, the banking system is so unreliable that a thousand-year-old system of money exchanges and forwarding services is used. This is particularly true in countries where civil strife or wars create large numbers of refugees. Some of the dislocated population settle in the West where their earnings are in hard currencies. To send money home to help their families, they can go to a corner store or a walk-up and entrust money to the operators who are usually from the same country.

In India and in the old Indian Princely states, the system was known as *hundi*, and more recently in connection with Afghanistan, the name *hawala* (to change, in Arabic) has crept into our vocabulary. The word *hawala* is now known as Islamic banking. Before e-mails, telexes, and modern communications, some of this money was sent directly to the country in the form of a chit, or *hundi*, which was redeemable in the country of origin of the sender. The fees charged for this service covered the risks and provided a profit for the operators.

Recently Pakistani expatriates working in the United Arab Emirates have been advised by the Pakistani Embassy to send their remittances home directly through legal banking and exchange channels. According to the press release issued by the embassy, remittances through *hundi* or *hawala* are illegal. Yet still we read about people who are detained by the customs service because they have undeclared sums of money in their possession.

A lot of the African diamonds are smuggled and laundered into the legitimate market, and terrorists make handsome profits in the process.

Many intelligence organizations consider these nonbank systems a source of funds for terrorists. Other sources are criminal activities, extortion, diamond and people smuggling, and disgruntled nations and individuals. A lot of the African diamonds are smuggled and laundered into the legitimate market, and terrorists make handsome profits in the process.

• • •

Closer to home, the seeds of resentment are manifested differently. In most states if a trooper pulls your car over and asks for your driver's license, the police cruiser will have a radio or computer terminal to verify your details. The officer will know if you are wanted, have outstanding parking tickets, or are a deadbeat dad. As a result, over a dirty taillight you could end up with major immediate headaches. Today when you apply for a job, the prospective employer routinely checks with one of the credit bureaus to see how stable you are. Then because of the so-called War on Drugs, more and more people have to piss on demand.

On top of everything else, almost any federal agency can tie together your Visa charges, municipal tax records, voters registration, Social Security files, utility bills, and it knows more about you than your mother. Such knowledge can easily lead to control. *Control is what many people fear from the twenty-first century.* Is it any wonder that conspiracy theories abound, and there is a feeling of paranoia among us? However, increased control is required to combat terrorism. This dual purpose begets the formation of homegrown terrorists bent on eliminating controls and a return to nineteenth-century individualism.

It seems that when economic times are hard, the majority of citizens in any country show very little tolerance of those who are different. Part of this may be explained by human nature. We always seek a scapegoat for the troubles we are in. Looking in the mirror and facing the consequences of our actions can be very painful. Whatever the reason, higher unemployment rates in most of the nations in the developing world lead to isolationist pressures and adds to the woes.

Americans view many of the international organizations, like the United Nations, World Bank, International Monetary Fund, World Trade Organization, Organization of American States, and the International Telecommunication Union, either as a waste of money or a threat to American sovereignty. There are many so-called men in the street who would like the United States to return to a pre-World War I isolationist policy. Being global traders, the U.S. can't turn the clock back. A prime example is the aircraft industry exporting huge amounts of its products worldwide.

Over the last few decades, government institutions and agencies have assumed an increasing share of the costs involved in bringing up children. And though many parents have willingly handed over this responsibility to the state, they overlook the inherent dangers involved. Allowing the state to foot more and more of the bills for child rearing invites the state to assert and exercise an imagined right of control over children.

The media's monopoly is challenged by Net surfing. The creation of the Internet is so polarizing that we only now realize the potential it has.

Those surfing are the insiders, exposed to knowledge and information from all corners of the globe, and those without Internet access are the new poor. They are information poor. This is only a small part of the emerging cyberspace. This bioelectronic environment links people, telephone wires, fiber optic lines, coaxial cables, and electromagnetic waves.

In this environment, knowledge and incorrect knowledge exist side by side with data in electronic format. Most of this knowledge is specialized, customized, and temporary. All of this data is accessible only to those with the right keys. Thus those left out are not able to compete with those with access. We are widening the gulf between the haves and the have-nots. Current estimates state that up to 50 percent of the population have Internet access. This trend in cyberspace sounds the death knoll of huge centralized institutions.

What about the developing nations? We see the emergence of criminal anarchy in many countries. People are facing displacement through internal and external events, unprovoked crime, erosion of nation states and international borders and the rise of private armies. Disease is rampant and overpopulation threatens the scarce resources. In many of the African countries, the government controls the cities and countryside during the daylight hours only. The armies are unruly rabbles who extort money and goods from all and sundry.

Terrorism is the poor man's way to resist superpowers. This statement is not in support of terrorism. It is a sober conclusion drawn from looking at world events. Our policy of "gunboat diplomacy" has served to worsen the social and economic conditions that I have discussed. Terrorist organizations have been growing for years, and on September 11th they struck their first major blow, thrusting us headlong into a New World Disorder.

2
A NEW WORLD DISORDER

"If there is anything which it is the duty of the whole people to never entrust to any hands but their own—that thing is the preservation of their own liberties and institutions."

—Abraham Lincoln

Nearly two years have elapsed since September 11, 2001. Are we safer today? Yes and no. For months after the event, we were on high alert. We captured the home base of al-Qaeda, but now we are relaxing. This is akin to what military commanders call battle fatigue. A favorite tactic used by the attacking force is to keep the defenders on high alert. This is accomplished by a few artillery salvoes, overflights by reconnaissance planes, and other actions designed to make the opposition believe that attack is imminent. Done long enough, the attackers will face a worn-out defender, thus increasing their chances for success.

We have been subjected to the same type of pressures. First we had hijacked planes used as weapons of mass destruction, then false alarms, and now a seemingly calm period. Many are saying, "We won, let us lie back and enjoy our victory." Some of the new security measures are ineffective at best and total shams at worst. Yes, we do have some sky marshals, but only enough to find one on every six hundred flights. Our senior bureaucrats seem to have a phobia about guns. Phobia or not, guns are the last line of defense in a hijack situation, and without them on board, our pilots are defenseless.

Clearly we have begun to relax. We even renewed the student visas of two of the long-dead hijackers. There was a proposal in the Oklahoma senate to deny flight training to noncitizens. Should we want to train Royal Air Force pilots, we better avoid Oklahoma. That will show them. Instead of focusing on what works, we fritter away precious time and resources on things that sound good.

For your safety in this new world, you can't afford to let your vigilance down. I do not propose extreme measures. I propose that you be aware of your surroundings and think about your actions. To give you an idea, many would laugh at the idea of hijacking a train, after all it runs on tracks. But what if terrorists take control of a train and use it as a battering ram in a station or freight yard? All they need are a couple of accomplices to flick some switches. You should be vigilant if the train is picking up speed where it usually slows. If you are aware of your surroundings and prepared for any terrorist attack, you will know that you can uncouple the cars from the rest of the train. The resultant loss of power brings the train to a halt and allows you to get off when it stops. You must be prepared for different scenarios during our new "war on terrorism."

Every incident, terrorist related or not, results in flooding the area with security, fire, and medical personnel, leaving other areas with little or no protection. I recall a story of a small bomb exploding next to a medical clinic. The police arriving on the scene were the victims of a nasty surprise in the form of a second, more-powerful bomb. If I remember correctly, one officer was killed. As Murphy's Law teaches us, you must assume that everything that can go wrong will.

What can be used against us by terrorists and copycats? The answer is anything and everything. For example, take a look at cleansers and other household chemicals under the kitchen sink. Should you start mixing them, very soon chlorine gas will be released. At best this will drive you from your home. At worst it can cause lung impairment or even death. If you need instruction on how to make this deadly concoction, just read the warning labels on the containers.

There was a chlorine leak once in a pulp and paper plant where I worked. Being a very junior employee, I was brown-bagging my lunch. As a result, I was the only one in the laboratory when the chlorine alarm sounded. I donned a full-scale industrial gas mask, dashed into the chemical control room, and turned off the main chlorine valve. I then dragged out the semiconscious operator. Time elapsed: perhaps thirty seconds. Once outside, I tried to remove the gas mask by grasping the filter and burned my hand. The mask got so hot that the paint was blistering and peeling off. We both received oxygen, and today it serves as a reminder that an emergency can strike at anytime.

I cannot emphasize enough that we must change our mind-set and be prepared for any possible attack. Even if the government severely restricts the purchase of chemicals, like sulfuric acid, which may be used in making explosives, we would still not be safe from a crafty terrorist with an elementary understanding of chemistry. Someone bent on mayhem but without resources could steal a few car batteries, break them open, and pour the weak sulfuric acid into a pan. Heating the pan until a dense white vapor is released (which is the water used to dilute the acid) will produce a concentrated sulfuric acid that can be used to make nitroglycerin.

A determined person will get what is required to carry out an attack. At the height of the Irish "troubles," agricultural potassium nitrate was coated to make it useless as a bomb material. The wily terrorists washed off the coating and went on making explosives as before.

Photo IDs are the rage today. But the truth is that most security people looking at them could not tell the difference between a Wyoming driver's license and a Guantanamo prisoner's library card. The bottom line is that legislation won't keep you safe, only preparation will.

• • •

The increased number of terrorist incidents forces greater collaboration between fire/police/EMS personnel and increasing cooperation with military agencies. However, terrorist events move faster than our ability to respond to them. This leads to decision makers being forced into making uneducated "guesses" about what to do next. The results are raids on the wrong households and sometimes arrest of innocent people. These hamhanded efforts are alienating parts of the population from the authorities.

At the same time, imagine the tension in lands subject to ongoing terrorism, not knowing whether the bus taking you to work will explode or a rabid fundamentalist will kill you because you are a tourist in some country beset by strife. In response, the people subject to the holocaust use retaliatory techniques even Himmler would have been proud of. This is the great contradiction facing us today. Living with these tensions, some individuals commit spectacular acts thus adding to the continuing strife.

If we have major earth changes, the wealthy nations will be blamed. We

> *Are we reaching the point where our offspring will not be able to say, "When we grow up," instead they will say "If we grow up"?*

may see the remaining whites being hunted down in African countries, an invasion from the Middle East and from the former USSR republics in Asia in the name of revenge. The most recent example of revenge killings was exhibited in Rwanda, Kosovo, East Timor, Congo, and in our own homeland. The ancient Romans annihilated all inhabitants of Carthage and salted the land so it would remain forever uninhabitable. We are not too different in outlook and reaction to those Romans, but we have more deadly salts.

Are we reaching the point where our offspring will not be able to say, "When we grow up," instead they will say "If we grow up"? This is just one of the issues we must contemplate in the new millennium. As we have seen through history, swords are not made into plows, they rust in storage while they are replaced with better swords. If you are trying to earn a living and believe that the terrorists operate in other lands, this was shattered as of 9/11. We must be aware of events in faraway places as the one thing uniting almost all of these groups is hatred of the U.S.A., our way of life, and our freedoms.

Terrorism and Tribalism

Modern terrorist movements are turning away from their communist or Marxist-Leninist roots and are increasingly based upon various religious beliefs. Real or imagined slights of the past are reasons to wage a war of terror on innocents who just want to pay their mortgage and credit-card debts.

The word "fundamentalism" has become almost synonymous with terrorism. In a religious context, fundamentalism simply designates a person or a group of people that believe in a strict interpretation of the basic tenets of their religion. Yet we have seen fundamentalists uttering their God's name before committing the most heinous acts. The leaders of terrorist organizations put on the cloak of religious fervor to gain supporters and to provide a convenient rallying point for the "troops."

All religions have factions, sects, splinter movements, and diverse leaders. Many are involved in terrorist activities. For your safety, you have to be aware if there is a place of worship or large number of people from a militant sect in your neighborhood. If so, there will be some activity sooner or later. It could come in the form of increased police presence, fire, or even bombings.

In order to understand what part religion plays in terrorist threats, we must have a better understanding of the major world religions. The three major religions of the world can all be traced back to Abraham. He is said to be the father of two great nations, the Hebrews and the Arabs. Perhaps the current conflict between Israel and Palestine is so bloodthirsty because it is a fight between two brothers.

Judaism

Judaism is based upon Mosaic Law. The five books of Moses constitute the written Torah. Special sanctity is also assigned the Talmud, Midrash, and various commentaries. Among Orthodox Jews, almost all areas of life are governed by strict religious discipline. The emphasis in Judaism is on ethical behavior and, among the traditionalists, strict ritual obedience.

Judaism, like most religions, is not monolithic. There are splinter groups, sects, and fanatics. Some observe the Sabbath strictly while others are more secular. There are Orthodox groups who dress like they did after the Diaspora as well as reform sects who take a more modern approach to their religion. In common with other world religions, there is infighting among different groups, all saying that they are the only ones who will go to heaven. So unless you are a member of all religious groups in the world, your ticket to hell is already issued.

The belief in prophecy was the moving principle behind the establishment of the Israeli nation, carved out of Palestinian territory. To be a citizen of Israel, you must only prove that you are a Jew. As the Jewish population in Israel increased, the tension between Israelis and Palestinians increased exponentially. The establishment of Jewish settlements on the West Bank and other areas that were once Palestinian ignited the intifada, an uprising against Israeli advances in Palestine. Oslo Accord notwithstanding, the killing continues to worsen.

Christianity

Jesus Christ subscribed to Mosaic Law, but added to it compassion. This had the effect of gaining heaven by confessing and belief alone. Christianity has deified Christ by identifying Him as God's Son. Even in the mainstream Christian churches, a debate rages whether the rapture comes before, during, or after the prophesied tribulation. Like Jews, Christians believe in Mosaic Law, or as it is also known, the Old Testament. However, they also believe in the New Testament, which is comprised of scriptures from

Christ's disciples written in the years following his death. The two books of the Bible form the basis of Christian teachings.

Islam

The world's fastest-growing religion is Islam. Those who adhere to Islam are known as Muslims. Like Jews, Muslims believe in Mosaic Law, and like Christians, they believe that the prophet has arrived. However, Muslims believe that Muhammad was the true and final prophet. The basis of Islamic faith is found in a holy book known as the Koran, which Muslims believe was dictated to Muhammad directly by God.

Islam is very much a communal religion and includes public display of one's piety in prayer at fixed interval throughout the day. Mecca is the holy city of Islam, being the main home of Muhammad after enlightenment.

Islam has evolved into a liberal/conservative spectrum as commonly occurs with ideologies. As with the Bible, holy books are immutable, but interpretations may vary over time. An extreme case of interpreting the Koran resulted in destruction of historic monuments of Buddha by the Taliban leadership in Afghanistan.

• • •

In Muslim countries, we are seeing the "Islamic Domino Theory" at work. This newest spread of Islam began in modern times with the fall of the shah of Iran in the late 1970s. It has been called the "Islamic Revolution" and or just "jihad" by observers and followers alike. It involves an effort to spread fundamentalist Islamic teachings and adherence to Muslim philosophy throughout the world. Most analysts would agree that that, in and of itself, is not something ominous or threatening. It is a practice as old as religion itself. Historically most religions have attempted to export their beliefs to other countries. What is troubling, according to both theological and political experts, is the concept of allegedly using intimidation, violence, murder, and terrorism to further religious goals.

A study of recent history would suggest that there is evidence of an orchestrated Muslim campaign underway to attain both religious and political control of a number of countries on several continents. The leading and most extreme factions of this movement are undoubtedly found in Iran and Afghanistan. Other major components and financial supporters exist in Syria, Pakistan, Israel, Egypt, Iraq, Turkey, Lebanon, and parts of the former Soviet Union.

The facts of the past three decades adequately demonstrate that some Muslim extremist movements and groups have actively engaged in the use of shootings, bombings, assassinations, and other nefarious activities, reputedly in support of their religious faith, but more covertly in an effort to subvert other countries. Even though the Koran prohibits the use of unprovoked violence, some extremist mullahs and ayatollahs have interpreted other sections to justify and condone barbarous acts in the name of the Islamic struggle to gain more adherents and further territorial expansion.

Unless this is stopped, it is too likely that a raging beast of religious fervor could engulf and conquer as many as a dozen nations in the coming decade. This is happening at a time when foreign intervention (i.e., the Crusades) is passé.

The first conflict of the new millennium sets aside all our notions about war. Gone are the days of facing the enemies, defeating them, and signing a cease-fire in some convenient railroad car. It is clear that religious struggles have become a central part of the New World Disorder.

We are at war with a shadowy organization that uses hit-and-run tactics and suicidal fanatics to carry this war to us.

We are slaves of petroleum. Now that more than 50 percent of the remaining crude oil resources are located in the most-unstable lands of the world, we have a real headache. While we are not doing very much to reduce our dependency on petroleum-derived fuels, we are relying more and more on imported oil. The supplier countries are mostly Muslim nations, which believe that they are under siege by the non-Muslim world.

This explosive combination already has given us global terrorism, a race for terrorist nuclear devices, and a deep suspicion of Muslim minorities in the developed nations. All it would take is one spectacular incident to ignite the smoldering resentment by unemployed citizens in the developed nations to demand that the government take measures against the Muslim minorities. With extremists on both sides, this is almost certain to happen.

The al-Qaeda network declared war on America, professing religious reasons. We are at war with a shadowy organization that uses hit-and-run tactics and suicidal fanatics to carry this war to us. Once a deed is done, they disappear into the safe haven of Afghanistan, forcing us to mobilize our armed forces and cause economic hardship for many. By using major military intervention, Americans changed their foreign policy and helped rid the world of many al-Qaeda members and topple the Taliban in Afghanistan. However this has not changed the conditions that created the terrorists in the first place. Those conditions persist and could rear their ugly head in any number of places around the world.

Turkey's control of the headwaters of the Tigris and Euphrates rivers, and their current hydroelectric projects, give it control over Syria and Iraq. However, the Kurdish issue may change this. The water projects are in areas settled by Kurds. About half of the twenty million Kurds live in Turkey representing about 25 percent of the Turkish population. The outcome of the Turkish-Kurdish dispute could destabilize Turkey and Iraq, as well. In the name of pacifying the Kurdish areas, Turkey is slowly encroaching on Iraqi territory.

The question facing us is not whether there will be war, but what kind of war will it be? And who will fight whom? The old rules of state warfare do not apply to the future. For example, a cease-fire with one Bosnian commander was soon broken by another Bosnian commander. Then when you add the Chetniks in Serbia, the "technicals" in Somalia, the Tonton Macoutes in Haiti, the skinhead Cossacks, and the Juju warriors, you realize a whole new kind of warfare has emerged.

It will be a war of land mines, snipers, ethnic cleansing, and terrorism. As always, civilians will suffer. The distinction between war and crime is disappearing. At the same time, states and local governments in these lands are unable to protect their citizens physically—we will see subnational private armies providing this protection.

What can we expect from a world disorder? Initially, all would seem to continue as before with one important difference. Developed nations, such as the United States, have been so preoccupied with internal matters that aid to developing nations was ignored. This resulted in the destabilization of the governments of developing nations, which may ultimately lead us to use weapons of mass destruction to halt the migration of starving people to developed nations. We will see a flight of the professional class from these nations to the developed nations thus adding to the misery for those left behind.

Eventually the regression to savagery and tribal practices stabilize, leaving a wake of destruction in its path. However, you must be prepared if you intend to survive the coming revolution so that you, your children, and grandchildren can be part of the next age of exploration, so that they can repeat the vicious circle of exploitation and pillage. This seems to have happened before, and by the looks of it, it will happen again.

3
GLOBAL AND REGIONAL TERRORISM

"It is better to be violent, if violence is in our hearts, than to put on the cloak of nonviolence to cover impotence."

—Mohandas K. Gandhi

"Nothing is ever done in this world until men are prepared to kill one another if it is not done."

—George Bernard Shaw

The world has changed incredibly. We can never feel totally secure anymore. We live in an age of unprecedented changes. One of these is the ability of an individual or a small group of people to wreak havoc on the population. This ability, coupled with festering sores of tribalism, nationalism, and elitism, forces us to consider how to protect ourselves and our families from the effects of these new threats. These threats come in all types and sizes, but we are not completely defenseless.

Surviving terrorism on an individual level does not call for you to take on the terrorist groups by yourself. The state is there for that task. Surviving is about staying alive, period. This chapter was written for civilians, not unlike the ones who were victims of nerve gas attacks in Tokyo. We are the ones who have neither fancy isolation suits nor digital survey meters. We must get by with the supplies on hand should our local neighborhood terrorist decide to engage in some low- or high-technology mayhem. The first step to survival is understanding your surroundings.

• • •

Terrorism is as old as history. Therefore we should have plenty of information to understand current conditions. Historically a weaker state or group, knowing that in a head-on confrontation it will lose, will always resort to other means. These can range from sabotage and tax evasion to guerrilla warfare. Lump this all together and you have a very loose definition of terrorism.

At one time, with the two superpowers facing each other, survival measures were simpler. When the saber rattling escalated, you "bugged out." That is to say, you evacuated from the target areas. Now we have no visible escalation ladder to provide a warning time. We have no forewarning. While the threat is at a lower level, it is much more unpredictable. In the past, many knowledgeable people moved out of cities and took up a more pastoral lifestyle or moved to smaller cities and towns. Is this still a good protective measure? Not really, considering a terrorist can be found just about anywhere these days.

Now the United States is the only remaining superpower. At one time, disaffected groups and nations could play off the U.S. and Soviet Union so that neither superpower had much sway over their future. Today their impotence against our might builds to rage and is directed primarily against American targets at home and abroad. Often Americans are the ones singled out in "revenge" for real and imagined wrongs that may have happened even before the thirteen colonies united.

Terrorism is big business nowadays. We have all flavors of it. The religious right, the radical left, and the dislocated minorities are just some examples of potential terrorist threats. Generally there are four types of terrorism to consider: external, internal, race, and religious. To complicate matters, they often overlap.

There are also many different weapons in the terrorists' arsenal. Bombs are very bad soldiers. They do not distinguish between friendly and enemy units and kill indiscriminately. While governments call bombs the weapons of cowards, the practitioners of this type of warfare call it the "poor man's revenge."

However, bombs are only a small part of the terrorists' arsenal. There are other methods they use to create havoc such as: throwing a diseased animal carcass into a city's water reservoir, letting natural gas accumulate in an empty house and using a remote-controlled spark generator to ignite the gas, and blowing up electric grid towers.

Let us look at newspaper headlines from the past few years:
- Bombing of federal building in Oklahoma City
- Fringe group terrorizing small town
- Rail car derailment forces evacuation of village
- Atlanta Olympic park bombing
- Small-town woman dies of anthrax

Sarin nerve gas was used by a religious cult in the Tokyo subway. In all likelihood terrorists have obtained nuclear materials. There is a whole new class of terrorists out there. They are well educated, and many have a professional background. This is a new trend. Airplane hijackings and hostage taking are the ways of the past. Terrorists are moving up the learning curve. In the meantime, we on the North American continent must be ready to deal with new threats to our well-being.

It seems that modern-day terrorists have also moved, perhaps in search of a safe house, chemical factory, or training base. Now the terrorists are out in the villages and the countryside, living among those who, in search of security, fled the major cities. This forces us to rethink security. No place is safe anymore. Therefore, we must be aware of what counter-measures can be taken to protect against the effects of terrorism, and we must be able to take them wherever we are.

The external threat

Terrorism coming from other countries is the poor man's way of waging war on a powerful enemy. The Irish attacks in Britain are good examples of this type of terrorism. We've had some examples on this side of the Atlantic. The World Trade Center is but one of them. Offshore terrorist organizations send their members into the U.S. as tourists, students, or whatever. Once here, they go underground and establish safe houses for others, often illegal immigrants, from which to operate. Saudi Arabia, Lebanon, Germany, and France have suffered these attacks. They have even taken place on the high seas. Instead of the "fog of war," we now have the "smog of terrorism."

As time goes by, the nature of the terrorist threats is more identifiable.

Today security is enhanced. Because of the external nature of the threats, border security was increased to the point that auto manufacturing is suffering. Just-in-time delivery is just a lingering memory. Denials of racial profiling are for public consumption. Front-line screening agents will continue to pigeonhole groups of people as they are doing today with airline-boarding procedures.

Israel encourages the assassination of terrorist leaders. Once done, there is relative quiet until a new leader emerges. However, with an organization like al-Qaeda, bin Laden is more like the chairman of the board. Al-Qaeda has a dispersed leadership structure. Therefore if Osama bin Laden or his designated successor, Ayman al-Zawahiri dies, the organization will continue. The word al-Qaeda means "the base." The organization brings together a number of terrorist groups and forms alliances with others.

There are also terrorist sympathizers to contend with. They are not active terrorists, but they will, because of political beliefs, ethnic background, or other reasons, provide aid to terrorists. These people are very difficult to identify. They may be Americans, and unless they have a terrorist history, they are practically invisible to counterterrorism officials.

The counterterrorist agencies are spread quite thin, and some people bent on malfeasance escape their attention.

The Border Patrol is facing increasing threats. At one time, it had to deal with economic migrants in search of jobs. Now there are shooting targets tacked onto the fence along the U.S./Mexico border. The targets have a Caucasian officer's silhouette and many holes shot through them. Then there are the very sophisticated transmitters confiscated in the southwest portion of the border. Whether this is associated with drug runners or foreign terrorists is irrelevant. Both are aimed at penetrating the United States.

Islamic extremists pose an increasing terrorist threat. For example, following the life sentence handed out to Sheik-Abdel Rahman for his part of the World Trade Center bombing in 1993, many fatwas (religious orders) were issued to exact revenge against America. These led to a call for a jihad against the United States. Security was increased at airports, embassies, and businesses, both at home and in foreign countries.

International terrorists do not congregate exclusively in New York and Washington. They can be found in rural settings as well. This increases the problems facing the agencies engaged in the fight against terrorism. The counterterrorist agencies are spread quite thin, and some people bent on malfeasance escape their attention.

Finally, even our government realized that we are under attack by foreign-based terrorists. The result has been the persecution of those nationals living on American soil, thus providing a fertile recruiting ground for the real terrorists. To provide better information for counterterrorist activities, the Department of Homeland Security was established. This was done to bring together information collected by the FBI, CIA, NSA, INS, local and state police forces, and others. It is hoped that this new department will end the turf war between security agencies.

The public sentiment against the terrorists in the U.S. will have an international impact. In some countries, people will make life miserable for Americans traveling there. Americans working for international aid agencies have been targeted by terrorist sympathizers. U.S.-owned businesses in foreign countries will be targets of local terrorists and want-to-be terrorists.

The Internal Threat

Seeing the Oklahoma City's Alfred P. Murrah Federal Building blasted into rubble served as a wake-up call for all of us. Domestic terrorism is a fact of life now. Previous terrorist acts went almost unnoticed, but the loss of life in blowing up the federal building could not be ignored. The American scene is replete with frustrated groups giving up on the judicial process. They are ready to take the issue directly to the so-called oppressors. In the past, we dealt with the perpetrators solely through the criminal justice system. Now it is more complex.

Part of the problem comes from the increasing powers of the federal and state governments. The old-time eccentrics now have become potential terrorists. It seems that the more pressure put on the population to conform, the less nonconformist behavior the authorities can tolerate. This is a rude reminder of the second law of thermodynamics.

Mind you, we have had internal terrorism before. Back in 1977, a Senate judiciary committee held secret hearings looking into sabotage attempts on pipelines, plans for hijacking an offshore oil platform, and an attack on a refinery. These terrorist activities were hushed up by the authorities to discourage copycats. Almost twenty years later, contingency planning to deal with terrorists is still inadequate. Except for some efforts by the FBI, we are reactive rather than proactive. That is, we will want to shoot the horse after it has bolted from the barn.

Because of the pressure on law enforcement agencies to control terrorism, police intelligence agencies will keep files on all types of people. These terrorist profiles will be all encompassing. For example, undercover officers are regularly fingered as terrorists by the terrorist profiles used. To compile these profiles, the government will use various databases.

What might get you on the list would be the purchase of four SKS carbines from your local gun dealer and filling out of the BATF forms, the phone call you made to Aunt Lucy while she was in Lebanon, the Visa charge at Wal-Mart for 500 rounds of ammunition, the MasterCharge slip for the fifty pounds of garden fertilizer from Joe's Garden Supplies, your membership in the NRA, your subscription to the *New American*, the fax you sent to the German government protesting the shipment of nuclear waste to France for reprocessing...and these are just a few. If you knew how much information the National Security Agency has on you, you would have an unrelenting Advil #10 headache.

There is also terrorism by groups and organizations for animal rights, nuclear disarmament, against the World Trade Organization, and other similar causes. Their tactics of direct action include tree spiking, pelt painting, product contamination, spring-loaded center punches on windows, glass-etching fluids, rooftop demos, breaking and entering, masking scents against hunting, damage to vehicles, bringing false charges against people, "ethical" theft, and "ethical" shoplifting. (Of course, "ethical" theft and shoplifting are nothing but self-justification for the criminal acts. Stealing from a mink farm is still stealing.) These are mostly small-scale, sporadic events, but they can be threatening to people living in the target areas.

High-tech terrorism

The Tokyo subway and sarin nerve gas incident proved that not all terrorists are stupid or without technological training and skills. If nothing else, this brought home to governments around the world that they should not alienate technically trained people. Japan controls the ownership of firearms, as do many other nations. However, you cannot control knowledge. In many cases, hi-tech terrorism is made possible by state sponsorship. State sponsorship provides a safe training area and supply base for the hi-tech terrorists.

Other forms of hi-tech terrorism are planting computer viruses, breaking into data banks, and sabotaging data storage archives. Hackers are an archetype of hi-tech terrorism. A good hacker in the National Security Agency computers can make you the archbishop of Canterbury or a wanted child molester. Even the low-level sabotage of plugging receptors for credit cards can be disruptive. When this is coupled with an ambush (a stationary raid) of the service personnel coming to repair it, it can be really vexing to the authorities.

What is the definition of hi-tech terrorism? The definition is twofold. Most people think of using products of current technology as high-tech terrorism. This is only partially right. High-tech terrorism also includes using low-tech means to disrupt our hi-tech society. What would these include? At one extreme, it could involve an animal rights group claiming to infect Thanksgiving turkeys at your local supermarket with botulism and at the other end, shooting at the small hornlike devices of microwave relay systems.

> *The Aum cult had sufficient chemicals to manufacture six tons of nerve agents and the ingredients to produce botulism toxin.*

For example, let us look at the perpetrators of the Tokyo subway attack. The Aum cult had sufficient chemicals to manufacture six tons of nerve agents and the ingredients to produce botulism toxin. It had made attempts to obtain the Ebola virus, had tested sarin on sheep in Australia, and was planning a coup in Japan. It also possessed a war chest in excess of $300 million, a Russian helicopter, and two unmanned drones as a delivery system. The Aum's membership was 10,000 in Japan and 30,000 in Russia, and it had ties with North Korea.

Because our society is so complex, it does not take too many terrorist acts to disrupt it. Major disruptions will have a domino effect. Twenty-first century technology will be coupled with first-century human reactions. There is also the fear of a terrorist act. This fear by itself will cause a major change in our lifestyles. This may result in poorly attended public meetings, reducing the participation of people in the democratic process. This would enable a small number of activists to hijack the governing of an area.

If you hear about the hijacking of a French plutonium shipment destined for Japan, a loss of Russian nuclear warheads, or that a group has carried out a biological test on some animals, then you know that acts of high-tech terrorism are very close. For years, we have been hearing about people breaking into government computers through the telephone. They are called hackers. Until now, this has not been an organized form of terrorism, but that can change.

We already have some evidence of the so-called Class III Information Warfare. Electromagnetic pulses, logic bombs, and HERF (High Energy Radio Frequency) guns enable hi-tech terrorists to bring the computers of banks, financial houses, and trading organizations to a halt. This was already demonstrated in England by successful extortion of at least four banks. What a wonderful way to finance a revolution! On a larger scale, this could be an electronic Pearl Harbor and may lead to a denial of service by the financial community.

A proliferation of surveillance devices will accompany all government efforts to fight terrorism. However, if hi-tech terrorism breaks out, we will also see all kinds of sensors and warning devices on the market. Entering government buildings, corporate headquarters, and sensitive installations may require passing though metal detectors, explosive-sniffing devices, and multiple identity checks. To give you an idea of what can be done, read some well-developed fiction stories dealing with this kind of terrorism, ones that will provide you with a starting point for what awaits us.

We have had spectacular, but localized incidents, grab the headlines. Open warfare between nations may be replaced with hi-tech urban warfare. It is much cheaper and pays just as handsomely in propaganda headlines. In the future to see if this is the start of a campaign, you must figure out if there is a pattern to the events. The more patterned the attacks are, the more likely that a state-sponsored organization is carrying them out. The hi-tech nature of terrorism will result in additional controls on scientific research and activities. This will result in more and more government controls on technology-related activities.

Religious Wars

This section is under the heading of terrorism in spite of the word "war." When you look at religious conflicts around the globe, you will find that most of them are conducted like an old-time rumble. That is, thugs beat up unarmed populations and occasionally fight with other thugs. Osama bin Laden attempted to turn the hunt for him into a religious cause. Involving Muslim nations in a fight against terrorism has abated this attempt in the Afghan conflict but it's not over yet.

> *For many years, the United States government has been played like a violin by the Israeli government, leading to the Muslim nations singling out the U.S. as Israel's armorer.*

Currently, we see Jews versus Muslims, Christians versus Muslims, Catholics versus Protestants, and so on. The problem with these conflicts is that sometimes they spill over to America. This occurs when certain population groups are singled out in the U.S. because of a conflict in their ancestral land. Look at the treatment of American Arabs during Desert Storm. Just remember, it was Iraq who attacked Kuwait. The attacker and the attackee were both Muslim nations. The September 11 attack on America was a most vivid reminder of this trend of exporting conflicts.

For many years, the United States government has been played like a violin by the Israeli government, leading to the Muslim nations singling out the U.S. as Israel's armorer. The attack on the U.S. Marines in Lebanon was one manifestation of this. In turn this can lead to the persecution of people of that faith in the U.S. This scenario may arise out of another Jewish-Muslim confrontation.

Another type of religious war is the "Millennium War," and it is very likely to happen; this has precious little to do with the new millennium. The question we must ask is on what scale will this be. Many people believe that we have all the signs of the second coming of Jesus Christ or, as some refer to it, the end-times. Most people base this belief on the Bible, in particular the Book of Revelations. Some of the best minds in the country are arguing whether Christians will go through the tribulation (a seven-year period) part way through it or not at all. Whatever the case may be, this millennial event will spawn a host of factions within the established churches, and we will see the emergence of new sects, as well.

Some of these sects will have leaders of questionable character. Unfortunately, since many people will follow anyone in search of belonging and understanding, they will fall prey to demagogues. Conflict between sects may be localized. But a skillful orator could fire the public's emotions, leading to the emergence of a nationwide movement.

Extreme positions will be taken, and there will be no quarter given to any in the opposing camp. It may even come to the anecdotal story about the mayor of Belfast being kidnapped by one faction of the Irish movement. Upon being asked what religion he was, he replied that he was a Jew. Whereupon he was asked if he was a Catholic Jew or a Protestant Jew. That could happen here, too. No matter how you look at it, religious wars, along with race or minority wars, are the most vicious and destructive conflicts.

Recently we have heard of black churches and Muslim places of worship being destroyed by arson. This does not constitute a religious war. Religious war occurs when two groups are so divided that intermarriage between the two constitutes a hazard to the lives of the newly married couple.

Presently there is a real threat to fundamentalist Christian and Muslim religions and sects. Christian churches and Muslim mosques are under attack, and the people belonging to these churches seem unaware of this. Lately they are being infiltrated by federal agents. This is even-more likely if they are outspoken critics of the status quo.

If the situation continues to deteriorate, there could be a real conflict between two religious groups. Such conflicts usually start with fights among the youth elements. Some religions are more likely to be targets of religious warfare because of how the public perceives them. We will hear about fierce Muslims, wily Jews, godless Buddhists, and so on. These convenient labels will be applied as the fires of hatred are fanned. Even religions that have been perceived as pacifist will be involved. When you hear of Quakers taking up arms, you know something is really brewing out there.

Depending on where you live, it may become hazardous to your health to practice your religion. Many of the Jews in Portugal seemingly converted to Catholicism in the fifteenth century to save their lives. You may want to read up on the period to know how they coped. It is a lesson in survival.

About this time, the participants of the religious confrontation will form "laagers," or encampments, around which wagons are circled for protection. Others will quietly blend into the background by giving up participation in the activities of their religions. There will be headlines about freedom of religion, but the actual deeds will be a signal for less and less religious tolerance. Some clergy or mullahs will become victims of the conflict, creating instant saints and martyrs.

The government will have to intervene to protect the losing side. This will bring accusations by the other side of favoritism. There will be some restrictions on freedom of assembly. Once again, the government will be blamed by both sides.

This is when you must make decisions. Before you do that, take stock of your loyalties. Logically, your loyalty should be to your God, your family, your neighborhood, your town or county, your state, your country, and then your race. Note that I did not mention religion anywhere. Both the Christian and Muslim faiths preach love and tolerance. We find neither in our present-day religions. More wars have been fought and people killed in the name of Jesus or Allah than anything else. Our religions have been politicized and have become a form of big business. So evaluate any religious conflict with the cynical eyes of a would-be atheist.

The authorities may permanently station troops to separate the warring factions, a la Northern Ireland. Once again, the efficiency of this separation will partially depend on the religious background of the troops and their leaders. No matter what line the government takes, the execution will be in the hands of government employees who may or may not have strong religious convictions.

The religious conflict may spread across the nation. You may see shipments of arms, ammunition, and other supplies from people to shore up their besieged fellow believers. This will further spread the conflict. You might have Catholic states squaring off against Protestant states. This lack of tolerance will extend to schools, workplaces, and even to community organizations.

If the warfare continues, the government could prohibit some religious practices. Woe to you if you belong to one of these religions. The gap between religious groups widens as the conflict drags on. The banned religions will go underground, and its members will be even further isolated from the mainstream population.

The Constitution notwithstanding, we shall see the government involved in religious affairs. This can range from licensing churches all the way to banning certain religions.

Rat Packs

Today we make a distinction between warfare and crime. But a few centuries ago, the one merged imperceptibly into the other. The distinction between common criminals and the armed forces of an invading state was entirely academic. Rape, murder, and plunder resulted inevitably from a visit by either.

In the Middle Ages, there was no such thing as a local police force. Occasionally, there were hired night watchmen whose job was to stay awake while others slept. But by and large, it was the entire community that undertook the suppression of crime by apprehending criminals whenever they were discovered. The real threat came from outside marauders and to counter that ever-present danger, there were expandable armies.

Traveling in Italy, you will pass by many villages perched on high peaks. These are Italy's famous hill towns, constructed during the Middle Ages to protect civilians from freelance marauders. Tens of thousands of landless cutthroats were brought together by the fourteenth-century wars between England and France. During the years of truce, unemployed mercenaries roamed Europe forming private armies that plundered and extorted from any community in their paths. The hill towns are monuments to the terror the mercenary armies inspired and to the peasants' determination to protect themselves the best they could.

Similarly, a number of French towns were built high on a bluff as a defense against raiders and rat packs. In the days of dirt roads, it would have taken a peasant with an ox cart an hour to go to his work. The French town of Domme was erected in response to Vikings coming up the

Dordogne River from Bordeaux. The high bluff gave the residents plenty of warning of approaching miscreants.

Today there are two forms of rat packs. The first is the familiar inner-city gang. The second is the outlaw gang preying upon available resources in rural areas. Let us take a quick look at how to identify them through their activities. They come in all flavors. There are the traditional prison gangs, motorcycle gangs, and Crips and Bloods. There are more recent packs, such as the Chinese triads and tongs, Jamaican posses, Cuban gangs, Vietnamese street gangs, Japanese Yakuza, Columbian drug cartels, and Russian Mafia.

There is a well-established tendency for the young of our species to form themselves into small, tightly organized peer groups or gangs. Once formed, they establish, within the existing social network, territorial rights to a particular area, in much the same manner as adults, since the territorial sense of acquisition is strong in all of us.

Even with the increase in the size of metropolitan areas and the accompanying increases of slum and ghetto areas, available gang territory is rather limited. One tangible result of this lack of space has been gang wars, or rumbles, between opposing gangs. These result in very high injury and mortality rates among the participants and even the bystanders.

The rural outlaws are similar to rat packs. The difference is that they are more mobile; bikers are an example of this. Criminal gangs gathered about the armies during World War I and II, Korea, and Vietnam. There are many such groups operating in Third World countries. Somalia and Liberia are two recent examples. They are even-more prevalent in areas receiving massive aid from developed countries.

It would be dangerously stupid to ignore the existence of such groups. Warlords may be leading the rat packs. A warlord emerges to provide protection for his area when weak governments cannot control areas of a nation. These warlords, in effect, set up regional governments.

To illustrate further that even small towns are not safe anymore, all along the rural corridor that parallels Interstate 95 from Florida to New York, Jamaicans have cornered the crack network. Small Town, U.S.A., offers easy profits to drug dealers at low initial risk because rural communities lack the drug awareness of big cities and are even less prepared than their urban counterparts to cope with naked savagery. Local police forces can be easily overpowered and even-more easily corrupted.

To give you an idea of the magnitude of this, take Florida. In Florida, the multibillion-dollar drug business dwarfs all other industries, including agriculture and tourism. In areas like South America, Pakistan, and Afghanistan, where cocaine, marijuana, heroin, and opium are produced, the drug dealers are better armed and equipped than the armies and police forces that are expected to control them.

Rat packs form due to crises. At first you are not affected. You will read about vicious gang fights breaking out. The death toll will be very high during these gang fights. The recruiting ground for rat packs is among the children of the poor. The day welfare checks are cut back, we will see a vicious trend emerging among the young in the poor sections of the cities. You will not be unduly concerned at first as the gangs are doing in each other, not the general public.

Ironically, self-help law enforcement is more likely to enhance civil liberties than continuing the status quo. Unchecked, drugs will threaten our civil liberties and rights to privacy because they are bringing us to a world where everyone must urinate for everyone else on command. Once we get used to that, additional intrusions into our privacy and civil liberties will be accepted as matters of course.

Compounding this is the problem of police corruption in this country. In the old days, many policemen were on the payroll of gambling establishments. Today, with increased drug profits, we find an even-larger police involvement in crime. Drug money finances many a poor country's public services, and in this country, drug money finances larger police department budgets. How so? When you declare war on drugs at a cost of $100 billion a year, the last thing your DEA agent wants is an end to his career by winning that war on drugs.

> *Be careful in all your dealings with authorities. Your assets can be confiscated under RICO and other laws.*

In times like this, be prepared to defend your home. Learn to shoot, and practice to maintain skill with firearms. Learn about the use of cover, the techniques of home defense, and the nature of the threat. Be careful in all your dealings with authorities. Your assets can be confiscated under RICO and other laws. All it takes is an allegation that your money came from drug dealing. Complaining to police internal-affairs people is like asking the goats to guard the cabbages.

If your neighborhood is the site of frequent conflict, place chicken wire on windows exposed to the street. This will keep out Molotov cocktails and homemade pipe bombs. About this time, the government will introduce curfews, and the police will patrol the affected areas in force. The gang fights will change in character. There will be widespread sniping and raiding. The local police will not be able to control the situation and will have to call on the National Guard.

Should you live in an area subject to the raids, your best bet will be to move for the duration. Even better, move permanently to a safer area of the country. The initial conflict will most likely be in the form of fire-bombings. This will force gangs to fortify their meeting places and to try to hide them.

The authorities will attempt to seize weapons from the gangs. They will also try to register and control all firearms in private hands. As always, this leads to firearms going underground. Instead of knowing who has what, the authorities will know even less. Remember, community law enforcement is the only proven method for controlling gang activities.

A black market in firearms will result in burglaries of homes of people known to own firearms. We may even see raids on police stations to obtain weapons. You may want to introduce a community patrol program. Use people who are volunteer firemen, little league coaches, and the like. Do not use thugs. Do not arm the patrols. Use two-way radios to bring help quickly. Obtain some kind of uniforms for the patrol. You should also carry insurance for the community patrol program.

As the situation worsens, the gangs will have carved out definite areas. These are no-go zones for the police forces, and even the National Guard will pull out at night. The borders of these gang areas will be marked by burned-out buildings and gutted vehicles. The people living in these areas will be held hostage by the gangs. The character of the conflict will change from raiding to a defensive posture. The gangs will try to protect their territories. Such a defensive posture will require very large forces to dislodge gangs. The advantage is usually with the side defending.

Many people will move out of the gang-controlled areas. The gangs will try to stop this movement. The reason is simple: If only gang members are left behind, then the armed forces will have an easier time identifying them and cleaning up. The armed forces will stage house-to-house searches. These can be very violent. If the armed forces casualties are high, you may see raids by armored vehicles that will fire at any sign of life. As usual, the innocent will comprise the majority of the casualties. Anyone admitted to a hospital with a gunshot wound will have some explaining to do. The number of detention camps will increase as the violence continues.

The police will pull out of gang territories. This will encourage the gangs to set up territorial, warlord-type governments. The warlords may or may not provide protection for the people living in their areas. The government, in desperation, may decide to use area weapons against gang-controlled zones. If this happens, even-more innocent lives will be lost.

The gangs will set up their own temporary governments in the areas they control. The government, in response, will mobilize the reserves to combat the rat packs. These engagements will bring the use of armored vehicles in gang-controlled locations. The gangs can defend only urban areas, where armored forces are working at a disadvantage. The rural gangs will have been eliminated by this time. Dispersed, they may make for the cities or wait until the army pulls out.

The government will occupy the gang areas with regular troops. The gangs will disperse and take up residence in other areas, starting the cycle all over again. Since the government has limited resources, the gangs may trickle back to their former territories.

As a reaction to the gang wars, the government will enact new laws and regulations. These will limit the number of people congregating at a place. (Religious worship may be exempt, in which case we shall see the formation of ".44 Magnums for Christ" congregations.)

4
PREPARING FOR A
WAR ON TERROR

Search of the caves in the Tora Bora Mountains in eastern Afghanistan uncovered many plans and materials the al-Qaeda organization was set to use. Among these were:

- Detailed plans for electronic initiation of dirty nuclear devices
- Recipes for large-scale chemical and biological warfare agent production
- Detailed systems for acquiring new identities or theft of others' identities
- Methods of training for suicide missions
- Detailed plans for industrial sabotage
- Plans for denying utility services to large population centers

Where to go? What to do? These are the questions facing a person confronted with the possibility of high-tech terrorists in Mr. Rogers's neighborhood. There is no place to go, but there is plenty you can do to protect family and friends.

First and foremost, have a plan of action. This plan must be made during the cruel light of day, facing up to the unappetizing choices available to us. You must have information, which can come from your scanner radio, your radiation-detection instruments, or by word of mouth. But information you must have. This is vital. Without information, you will be preparing for events not even remotely connected to what is happening in your area.

You must also have supplies on hand to wait out the danger period, which can range from a few hours to a few weeks. Once you have these supplies, you must know how to use them. The potential threats are not pleasant. And in a perfect world, we wouldn't have to deal with them, much less think about them. But what is perfect anymore? The potential for harm has migrated from the battlefield to the backyards of our nation. We cannot ignore it, for the powers that should protect us are completely unprepared to protect even themselves. As always, the individual must look after him or herself.

The preparation has its own timetable, but first you must evaluate your neighborhood and area. To start, ask the following questions:

- Am I living close to a transportation hub?
- Is my area near an international port?
- Would my area be a nuclear target?
- Is my area home to prominent people who may be target-ed by terrorists?

The answer is probably yes to one or more of these questions. Now what? Now is the time to take out the map of your area and decide what to do. First you must decide whether to stay where you live or evacuate. This is a very important decision. Evacuation is a must if your area is sub-ject to a nuclear blast. If you are faced with biological and chemical threats, you may be better off staying put.

Let me elaborate. Unless you have a five-ton truck, clear roads, and the fuel to get you to your destination, you may be leaving behind equipment and supplies that will make your existence easier. Most evacuations in the case of terrorist acts and chemical spills are for a short duration only. In the meantime, your possessions are at the mercy of the authorities, how-ever well-intentioned they may be. To top it off, the authorities will prob-ably have roadblocks channeling civilians into so-called reception centers. For better or for worse they will try to control your movement.

There are terrorist threats and actions all around us. Therefore, it is very difficult to tell when random events turn into an organized mayhem that threatens your way of life. The government generally has more infor-mation than the average citizen. When you see the government restrict vehicular access to certain buildings, when you are searched upon visiting a government office, when there are guards around water reservoirs, and when other measures come into force, you know that there is a definite threat out there. Rule number one for self-preservation is never become predictable!

Why is that? Well, imagine for a moment you are predictable. A terrorist can enter your residence, place a pound of black powder in your microwave oven, and set the timer for three minutes after your usual arrival time. Or take the light bulb out of your favorite reading lamp, file a small hole in it, fill it with black powder, and stick a piece of tape over it. When you turn the light on to read your newspaper, you will have a place in the next day's obituaries.

Architects are learning to cope with terrorist threats. Some of the steps they are taking include:

- Eight-inch base slabs with the supporting columns going all the way down to the foundation;
- Tiered buildings with tiered landscaping, to reduce the area subject to blast;
- Rebar in floors and ceiling laid in a crisscross pattern, with the rebar interconnecting with the rebar in the columns.
- No external ornaments that can fall off.
- Blast curtains and Mylar coating on the insides of all exterior windows.
- Reduced window areas to 20 percent or less and spacing columns closer together (twenty-five to thirty inches).
- All construction poured-in-place concrete with twelve-inch exterior walls and eight-inch-thick roof slabs.
- The employee parking to be at least 100 feet from the building and no underground parking.

In effect, the building is turned into a fort.

Many underground publications advocate the use of self-storage lockers to store arms, ammunition, explosives, drugs, and other substances. Police departments will set up surveillance and raid many of these self-storage establishments. Those remaining in operation will insist on verification of the identity of the would-be renter. Any person using such a facility will have his name on some list and probably will be questioned.

The U.S. government is taking steps to teach the countries supporting terrorists a lesson, as it did in Afghanistan. Call it a very powerful out-of-court settlement that sends a message to states supporting terrorists. The reprisals may work, depending on the sponsor country's nature. The terrorists may have religious as well as national overtones. This can turn the fight against terrorism really ugly. The U.S. will impose economic sanctions against the host country of the terrorists. The UN will be livid and will try to censure the U.S. on the basis of discrimination.

We expect that terrorists will step up their activities in the U.S. They will target government installations, hydroelectric dams, power transmission lines, rail yards, places where people gather, and anywhere where they can make the headlines. Terrorists seek media attention. This helps to keep their cause in the headlines and encourages the flow of money from sympathizers.

The terrorists plan to intensify their activities, now hitting any place where people congregate. There will be a number of symbolic targets, such as the Vietnam War Memorial if the terrorists are of Vietnamese origin. It is quite likely that local vigilantes will make attacks on neighborhoods with large concentrations of people originating from the terrorist country. This will result in widespread random violence.

Unless eliminated, continuing terrorism will lead to a complete elimination of our freedoms, meaning the terrorists will have won.

The Immigration and Naturalization Service will make raids on ethnic neighborhoods. These will result in the dispersal of people from the target area to other parts of cities. In some cases, this will lead to localized violence.

If the government's efforts to eliminate the terrorists are working, we may see easing of temporary restrictions. Unfortunately, as history has shown the many so-called temporary restrictions will become permanent. One has to look no further than the "temporary" income tax introduced during World War I. No matter which way it goes, the events will reinforce in the American psyche a mistrust of foreigners. Instead of a melting pot, we may become the practitioners of tribalism. This mistrust may create another terrorist movement among the legal immigrant population. It is likely that local police forces will also have to check on immigration status of people in their district.

One of two things will happen: Either the nation will be an armed camp with travel restrictions permanently in place, or the terrorist threat will have been eliminated. The terrorists may have gained the support of expatriates living in America, who will provide safe houses for them. This will make them very hard to eliminate. Unless eliminated, continuing terrorism will lead to a complete elimination of our freedoms, meaning the terrorists will have won.

PREPARING FOR A WAR ON TERROR

You can recognize that we are in a terrorist situation by not being able to park in the vicinity of a government building, by needing an escort to various offices, and by the searches of your briefcase. These are standard operating procedures in Ireland and other places beset by an internal terrorist campaign. Security will be beefed up at other locations as well, such as corporate offices and factories.

If you work for a large organization, it probably ran a security check on you. Its subcontractors will have their employees' backgrounds examined. Woe to one who espoused ideas contrary to current norm.

The government has given itself unprecedented powers for the "duration of the emergency." Phone taps without court orders and arrest and questioning of suspects without due process of the law are just two examples. Many people feel that this will be a vehicle for the "New World Order" to take over America. Time will tell.

Fertilizers, such as ammonium nitrate and sulfur, will have special coating substances added to reduce their usefulness for making explosives. There will be input-output balance forms to ensure that the purchasers do not divert their fertilizers into making explosives. Gunpowder may contain "taggants" to identify the source of the material. Sales of certain other chemicals will be severely restricted, and local police will follow up on local purchases to ensure that these are used for legitimate purposes. Woe be to you if you are a drag racer or a model-rocket enthusiast. Of course, the terrorist will happily use a solvent to remove the coatings from controlled substances, steal the supplies he needs, and continue as before.

To see if you are considered a potential terrorist, prepare a list of the organizations you belong to, your past associates, and your past purchases to evaluate if you would be on any of the governmental "special" lists. Do not joke about bombs or any other sensitive subject. You will find yourself under police scrutiny, even charged for a silly joke. Recently in Canada, an eighty-year-old veteran of WW II remarked to an airport security attendant, "Do you think my wife has a bomb in her purse?" He was promptly arrested, and it was not until days later, under extreme pressure from veterans and legal groups, that the charges were dropped. Other cases have much worse outcomes.

Additional government restrictions will be placed on the population in the name of law and order. As these restrictions are imposed, more resistance will be put up by the population at large. This will lead to even-more power being placed in the hands of the authorities. Of course, these will be strictly "temporary" in nature. Don't you believe it. Look at the introduction of the Social Security number. First it was only for Social Security. Now you can't even open a bank account without providing it.

If the random violence increases, there will be bombs exploding at public gatherings, and bomb threats will disrupt life in general. The authorities will respond with even-more controls to reduce access to government facilities. We may even see the emergence of a secret government. As science fiction author Henry Kuttner wrote, "Up till now, no race ever successfully conquered and ruled another. The underdog could revolt or absorb. If you know that you are being ruled, then the ruler is vulnerable. But if the world doesn't know—and it doesn't."

As internal terrorism increases, we may see the introduction of communist-era travel permits. You may need a travel permit to visit Washington and other major target cities. Border areas may require a special permit to visit, and the use of exit visas may be introduced to control who is leaving the U.S. and with what. If the situation degenerates to this point, many constitutional guarantees will be suspended. People will be held without charges. Preventive detention will enable those with grudges to get even by turning people in on trumped-up charges. We may even see use of a fine British invention used during the Boer War, concentration camps.

As terrorism increases, the list of proscribed goods will increase. You may find that your gardening activities will suffer due to the shortage of fertilizers. Moreover, making your own may result in bomb-making charges being brought against you. If you were considered an eccentric before, now you may be classified as a potential terrorist. Many innocents will be questioned and treated as terrorists. Roadblocks on major roads will be erected more and more frequently. They may become a permanent fixture on some major roads leading to large cities.

The authorities will try to curtail terrorist activities by profiling even-more people. The criteria will be so loose that anyone with a grudge will be able to turn in someone else. The neighborhood snitch program will be in full bloom. These measures will not reduce the terrorist threat since by now any eccentric will know that he is targeted by the authorities. The government's actions will serve only to increase unrest. There will be widespread acts of minor sabotage aimed at the government, which in turn will spawn even-more repressive actions. The government unwittingly will have created a self-fulfilling prophecy.

Due to these repressive measures, many people will be driven into the arms of the terrorists. What started as a terrorist movement may become a liberation movement. That is, liberation from a police state and government tyranny. Unless terrorism is brought under control, we will see the emergence of a police state. Your rights and property will be at peril from new regulations and at the whims of the enforcers.

Because of the paranoia associated with hi-tech terrorism, many innocents will have their doors broken down at four in the morning, while others will be turned in by neighbors with old grudges. The government will give itself many additional powers to contain the threat. The search for the terrorists will be like the witch hunts of the 1950s. Should you be a target of such attention, your best bet will be to grin and bear the illogical attacks.

We already know that phone calls may be monitored. Even though the NSA does not have a mandate to monitor communications in the U.S., it has an arrangement with the Canadian communications establishment. That arrangement provides for exchange of information. This is very much like the cat-and-rat ranch joke. We feed rats to the cats. When the cats are bigger, we skin them and feed the carcasses to the rats. The cats feed rats and, the rats feed the cats. Very neat.

Already we see a potential police state emerging. The authorities may monitor the purchase of certain electronic components. The curtain of secrecy surrounding many hi-tech terrorist incidents will be torn open by spectacular incidents, such as a paralysis of the banking system. At this time the standard operating procedure when some high-tech incident happens is to attribute it to a computer glitch, operator error, and the like.

To continue their activities, the terrorists will hijack chemical, military, and other shipments. This would result in additional controls on and probably armed guards for those shipments. There will be a proliferation of new police agencies for transport, ports, and other transportation facilities.

We are already experiencing longer air travel times, partially because of the preflight security measures. If you take a flight, expect to have your identity verified, your name checked in a computer network, your baggage, your shoes, and body searched before boarding. Roadside checkpoints will be a daily occurrence. If you travel, give yourself extra time for security checks en route.

> *After a bout of hi-tech terrorism, no one will feel safe, and government controls will continue indefinitely.*

Detaining many people suspected of being terrorists or terrorist sympathizers may reduce terrorist activities. However, after a bout of hi-tech terrorism, no one will feel safe, and government controls will continue indefinitely. A greatly revised terrorist profile will emerge. Woe to you if you are a well-educated person from a country suspected of supporting terrorists.

SURVIVING TERRORISM

We may see scientific research limited to people deemed to be patriotic. Those considered extremists will see their livelihood terminated. This may result in a cottage scientific industry. As in the past, most progress will come from these clandestine "garage" laboratories. As a precaution, review books in your bookcases. Any publication that can be construed to have a terrorist use, including old chemistry textbooks, should be cached in a safe place.

Society in the later stages would run from the top down, all in the name of security. A police state will emerge with all it entails. Freedoms will be curtailed and confiscation of private property will include homes and businesses from those suspected of sympathizing with the terrorists.

5
LIKELY TARGETS AND METHODS USED

I t cannot be said too often: the first line of defense against any threat is information. Get to know your neighborhood, the routes you take to work and areas where you spend a lot of time. Keep abreast of the national and international news. To give you an example, should war break out between India and Pakistan, you want to know if there are places of worship or other buildings where people from either country may congregate. That place may be a target if emotions are riding high.

After September 11, about a hundred high priority targets were identified in America. These range from centers of government to nuclear power generating stations. Too bad for anyone wanted by the police who goes by one of these installations. During heightened alert stages you can reasonably expect to have to prove your identity and explain your presence in the area. Depending on our adversary, the nature of these targets may change, but the White House is a tempting target to those wanting to humiliate the U.S.

Let us make a short list of what would be considered a target:

- government offices;
- power-generating and transformer sites;

- bridges and overpasses on major roads;
- military installations;
- dockyards;
- police stations and barracks;
- offices and plants of major defense contractors;
- warehouses and oil depots;
- oil and gas pipelines, in particular pumping stations;
- residences of high-profile people.

Obviously twenty-four-hour protection for all possible targets is impossible. This is where information is needed. Currently with the bin Laden crowd, these would be limited to where the maximum loss of life occurs and symbolic targets. After September 11, one does not have to surmise we now have stark evidence to know where these people want to hurt us. For example, a group from Indonesia would likely target offices of those companies with branch plants in that country.

Once religion enters the picture, the situation gets more ugly. We could see examples of Western architecture, places of worship, and even museums on the target list. Religious fanatics see the world differently from most of us. There is no compromise or tolerance. After all, that's why they are called fanatics.

Mindless violence begets retribution with many calling for the establishment of that wonderful British institution called the concentration camp where all people of the same religion could be incarcerated until the emergency is over. This will cut us off from valuable intelligence about the host country of the terrorists. Why is this so? People of Yemeni extraction can readily recognize someone else from that country. Should a Saudi steal the identity of a Yemeni, other Yeminis could finger him, making detection very much faster and possibly saving lives.

A prime example of religious targets is the Dome of the Rock. This Muslim holy place was built directly over the ruins of the Temple of Jerusalem. According to Scripture, the second coming of Christ will be when the temple is rebuilt. Many Christian and Jewish extremists are fervently praying for a well-placed earthquake in hopes of speeding up the return or according to some Jewish scholars, the first coming of the Messiah.

Worldwide there are a number of places and buildings whose symbolic value place them on a potential target list, some of these are:

- Mecca;
- the Sphinx;
- Beijing, Imperial Palace;
- the ruins of Petra in Jordan;
- Buckingham Palace;
- the Kremlin;
- the Vatican;
- Bethlehem;
- the temple in Salt Lake City;
- Taj Mahal, etc.

This short list provides a target for most of the terrorist groups and their sympathizers. Now that the New York World Trade Center is gone, many groups are contemplating attacks on symbols of their perceived enemies or oppressors. Being poor is no protection against being a target. Just think of the number of ma-and-pa shops in the neighborhood of the Twin Towers. A homeless person sleeping under a bridge is at risk if for some reason terrorists target it.

Although in the rich enclaves of gated communities the security forces could not defend against a determined attack, they would serve as a tripwire giving time for the authorities to arrive. All through history, we found that even the best security and intelligence operations can't adequately defend a target, but they are a deterrent to a casual attack.

Where do we go from here? The obvious answer is to keep out the terrorists in the first place, an impossible task as Americans and Britons were captured fighting on the Taliban side in Afghanistan. Although the movies depict the criminals as patriotic, reality shows that people who do things for money can be turned by the other side with more money.

You should view all places as targets. Some may be incidental. We have all heard about collateral damage in past conflicts. Our intelligence services, unless they penetrate the terrorist organizations, can't give us much warning, in most cases, no warning is given at all. Sometimes reading Nostradamus is more illuminating than reading intelligence reports, most of which are full of conjectures and sentences like "On the one hand, we believe that. ..."

6
BIOLOGICAL ATTACKS

"My definition of an expert in any field is a person who knows enough about what's really going on to be scared."

—P.J. Plauger, Computer Language, Programming on Purpose

"I think there is a very real danger that we're going to end up as a [world] society divided between those who were able to inform themselves first and those who were informed late. Those who have access to information and health care, and those who don't. Those who were able to change, and those who aren't. I think there is a very real danger of half of us turning into AIDS voyeurs, standing around watching others die."

—Renee Sabatier

This chapter is in two parts. The first deals with biological terrorism and naturally existing threats. The second part is the military application of military agents including decontamination. The recent anthrax attack resulted in a minimal loss of life, but in a major dislocation in our lives. To put it in perspective, the loss of life was less than what traffic accidents claim in the New York area in a week.

Experts are plenty scared today. We have new diseases; we have old diseases resistant to drugs. Formerly used pesticides are now deemed to be an environmental threat, and there has been a meteoric rise in the world's population. Sixty thousand deaths are caused each year in American hospitals from infectious diseases, and many of these are caught in the hospitals. One reason for drug-resistant bugs is that of the people prescribed antibiotics only 40 percent finish the full regime of the treatment. Keep in mind that throughout history infectious diseases have claimed more lives than wars, and today in the U.S.A., these diseases take more lives than car accidents.

To illustrate our vulnerability let us take a look at what happened in 1990 in the Swedish city of Linkoping. A patient was admitted with hemorrhaging fever, probably caused by a virus, and possibly a filovirus. (Ebola is also a filovirus.) The Swedish health system was taken unaware. It simply was not prepared for this kind of medical emergency. Even though there was a new safety laboratory at the Swedish Institute for Infectious Disease Control in Stockholm, the Swedes were not prepared to test blood samples from the patient.

The U.S. Army was called in. Staff and equipment were flown over from Fort Detrick, Maryland. The Americans reorganized the hospital quarantine and treatment routines. There was a fear of spreading the unknown fever. They were lucky in that the patient was not very contagious. They also had concerns about this being a terrorist attack. This happened in a nation well-respected for the excellence of its medical services. By the way, the patient survived.

What if there was an outbreak at several places at the same time? Fort Detrick has only a limited number of people and equipment to airlift around the world. The number of spacesuits worn by the staff and laboratory personnel involved in dealing with dangerous pathogens is also limited. This is one time when duct tape over aluminum foil just won't do.

These spacesuits are positive-pressure units with a battery-powered air supply. They are used in fieldwork with extreme biohazards that are believed to be airborne. The main body of the suit is disposable by incineration. The helmet and air blowers are designed to be easily disinfected. There are two versions in use, the Chemturion and the Racal. Your hospital is not likely to have one, perhaps a few may be found in any state. So medical personnel first coming into contact with some of these infectious diseases are likely victims themselves. These suits were used in Reston, Virginia, and in the Kitum Cave in Kenya (more on these under Ebola).

BIOLOGICAL ATTACKS

Dealing with many of these microorganisms you need a Biosafety Level 4 (BL-4) laboratory. Once again, these are found only in a few countries. The most famous is the one at the Centers for Disease Control (CDC) in Atlanta, Georgia. All outgoing air must pass through a HEPA filter, and there are air locks, reminiscent of a spaceship, for entry and exit.

These diseases are not likely to occur in Atlanta. Unfortunately, in the African countryside where many of these diseases are found, there are neither spacesuits nor BL-4 laboratories. There is an intense debate about what kind of protection is required. Even a prick from a needle would put hospital personnel at deadly risk. Given the poverty in these countries, use of disposable needles and syringes is not universal, and this adds to the problems.

What is most frightening is the emergence of pathogens resistant to antibiotics or even disinfectant. The most-alarming event concerned an outbreak of cryptosporidiosis (an intestinal parasite) in Milwaukee, Wisconsin, in 1993. The EPA laboratories found that the strain was living on Clorox. This kind of outbreak would be a death sentence to those with AIDS as their immune systems could not cope with the bugs.

One of the major causes of the spread of infectious diseases is travel. This was true in the past, and it is true today, except much more so. Aviation gave the bugs a wonderful new vehicle to visit the world and spread havoc on populations with no immunity. The European settlers did not wrest the continent away from Native Americans with guns, as some movies proclaim. No, their tools for taking the continent were smallpox, bubonic plague, measles, mumps, yellow fever, cholera, tuberculosis, and malaria. The isolated populations evolved from a relatively small gene pool and had no defenses against these weapons. It is estimated that out of a population of one hundred million, more than ninety million died due to diseases. Whole nations were wiped out.

Today with widespread travel, we are all more susceptible to infectious diseases. Dr. Joshua Lederberg, a Nobel laureate, said, "The microbe that felled one child in a distant continent yesterday can reach yours today and seed a global pandemic tomorrow." Throughout recorded history, human migration has been the path for spreading infectious diseases. Most new infections are not caused by new diseases. They are caused by the true-and-tried bugs that have been with us throughout history.

Crusades, wars, religious pilgrimages, military maneuvers, displaced populations, trade caravans, international commerce, explorations, and refugees played a central role in spreading diseases across the world.

Looking at some examples:

- We have already mentioned what happened in North America, as a return favor we got syphilis.
- Smallpox spread from India or Egypt around 1000 B.C. It then hit Europe. It moved into the Dominican Republic by way of Santo Domingo in 1518, killing one-third of the population, and then spread to other Caribbean areas.
- Plague is another good example. It was mostly found along trade routes in the past. It spread from Asia to Europe and then to California around 1900 and is still now rife mainly among wildlife.
- In 1994 Rwandan refugees fleeing to Zaire had a cholera outbreak, killing close to fifty thousand.
- In 1987 pilgrims from India and Pakistan carried meningitis to Mecca, Saudi Arabia, where they infected other pilgrims, spreading the disease throughout sub-Sahara Africa.
- People working in other countries and returning home are responsible for many of the modern epidemics.

> *Many of our transportation superstructures, which help rapid transit of goods and people, also assist microbes to travel at ease.*

Many of our transportation superstructures, which help rapid transit of goods and people, also assist microbes to travel at ease. Look around you at all the Interstate highways, bridges, tunnels, over- and underpasses, and ferries, and you will readily see what is meant. Then there are ships, discharging their bilge water, which is teeming with illegal "aliens" the Immigration and Naturalization Service (INS) can't see, let alone stop. The specter of wholesale population migration to the U.S. raised in Peter Brimelow's book, *Alien Nation*, pales in comparison to these microscopic wetbacks.

We are vulnerable in America because of our aging population, AIDS, people whose immune systems are suppressed for transplants, increased poverty, pollutants, crowding, stress, overuse and misuse of antibiotics.

Another form of vulnerability comes from the viruses' constant rearrangement of their genes, much like loose change, thus constantly creating new strains. Just look at the annual influenza outbreaks all needing new vaccines to combat them. One started in China where farmers raise pigs and ducks together. The avian flu virus from ducks infects the pigs, and inside the pig's cells, the virus swaps genes with mammalian viruses. The

BIOLOGICAL ATTACKS

1918 virulent flu virus apparently jumped directly from pigs to humans. However, this is only a hypothesis.

Changing lifestyles and more mothers in the workforce creates more problems. A much-greater proportion of children are in child-care facilities, day-care centers, and the like. These children are more likely to be exposed to hepatitis A, respiratory illnesses, parasites, and ear infections. These are then carried home and spread to other members of the household. The concentration of children in these facilities also provides an attractive target for terrorists.

Then we have the reemergence of infectious diseases like gonorrhea, malaria, and pneumococcal disease mostly due to microbial resistance to present-day antibiotics. Complacency on the part of public health services gave rise to the reemergence of TB, cholera, and pertussis. TB is the number one killer in the developing world.

Our early-warning systems are undergoing changes due to some of the bizarre diseases around the world. Yet at the same time, there is pressure on funding for these activities and downsizing in the health-care field. We will pay dearly for these shortsighted measures.

In addition to biological threats facing us in nature, we have history to guide us in its military use. Biological weapons have an inglorious past. During the Middle Ages, tribes engaged in desert warfare dropped plague-ridden corpses into the wells of their enemies. During the French and Indian War of 1763, the British infected the Indians with smallpox by giving them blankets that had been used by patients infected with the disease. Approximately 95 percent of the Indians who were exposed died of the disease.

During World War I, when horses were shipped from the United States to the Romanian cavalry, German agents inoculated these horses with the organism that causes glanders, a contagious disease of horses, communicable to man. In later stages of glanders, mucous membranes become inflamed, leading to ulceration. Until the development of antibiotics and modern medical practice, disease killed more soldiers than did actual combat. This was due to overcrowding, poor camp hygiene, inadequate medical support, and the physical stress of combat.

Today biological warfare has become another agent in the arsenals of many countries. For example a light plane flying over Washington, D.C., carrying 100 kilograms (220 pounds) of anthrax spores and equipped with a crop sprayer could deliver a fatal dose of up to three million people.

Let us take a look in more detail at some of the threats we are facing from these microorganisms.

Anthrax

Anthrax, the much-touted potential biological warfare agent, is getting increasing attention because of its potential use by Iraq. It's a bacterial disease that can infect all warm-blooded animals, including man. Up until now, it was an occupational disease, confined to those who are exposed to dead animals and animal products such as wool and hair. The infection is very rare in the United States.

The anthrax bacteria can live in the soil for many years. During World War II, Gruinard Island off the Scottish coast was used for experiments with anthrax. About ten acres were infected with anthrax spores. In 1987 the bacteria finally was eradicated from the soil and that was after treatment with large amounts of formaldehyde. Man may become infected by inhaling contaminated soil particles or by handling contaminated wool or hair from diseased animals. After the 1979 Sverdlovsk, USSR, accidental release of anthrax spores from a secret research establishment, crews moved in to remove the dirt and pave over alleys and playgrounds. Most of the crews used for this work died of anthrax.

The incubation period is around seven days. When symptoms appear depends on the type of exposure. With skin exposure, there is a boil-like lesion that eventually forms a black center. A swelling of the lymph glands close to the lesion may occur. With respiratory exposure, symptoms may resemble the common cold and may progress to severe breathing problems. The mortality rate is very high. Anthrax bacilli release a toxin damaging body tissues. There are no reports of anthrax spreading from human to human.

There is a vaccine available for people in high-risk occupations, and now members of the armed forces stationed in the Gulf region are vaccinated routinely. Anthrax is treatable in the first stage. The treatment is with penicillin G (50 mg/Kg) or tetracycline. Streptomycin has also been prescribed in conjunction with penicillin as it is synergistic. Today the antibiotic Cipro manufactured by Bayer is the drug of choice. The second phase of infection comes after a symptomless period and is characterized by shortness of breath, cyanosis, hypotension, and shock. This phase usually ends in death despite therapy.

In a biological warfare environment, anthrax spores would be disseminated as an aerosol, causing inhalation anthrax. As sunlight is toxic to most biological agents, this would normally be done at night. Particles one to five microns in size are most efficient in causing infection, and about three thousand particles lead to infection. For biological warfare, a penicillin-resistant strain of anthrax would be used. This is done by exposing anthrax germs to antibiotics and breeding the survivors. Then vancomycin is the treatment of choice. However, it's expensive and produced only in small quantities. Another problem arises from the protective suits that the disinfecting personnel must wear. On a hot day after fifteen minutes, almost no work is possible in these suits.

The anthrax used in the attack through our postal system is of a uniform-sized, pure strain. It has not been "militarized" in that it is not penicillin resistant. The attack hit Washington, D.C., Florida, New York, and probably other locations, as well.

Campylobacter

There are many forms of Campylobacter that cause disease in humans. *C. jejuni* is commonly present in healthy cattle, pigs, chickens, turkeys, ducks, geese, and wild fowl. It is also isolated from streams, lakes, and ponds. One recent outbreak in Australia has been tracked back to an uncovered rainwater cistern.

It was not recognized as a cause of human food-borne illness until 1975. Today, *C. jejuni* is considered the most common cause of food-borne illness in the U.S. and probably in the whole Western World. The vast majority of these is self-limiting and cause no more than mild to moderate diarrhea that lasts up to one week. Typical symptoms of more severe illness include severe abdominal pain, diarrhea, fever, nausea, headache, and muscle pain. The disease is rarely fatal (fewer than one per one thousand cases). However, this increases when other diseases (cancer, liver disease, and immunodeficiency diseases) are present. The incubation period is typically two to five days and lasts no more than one week.

Recent studies show that in rare cases Campylobacter may be linked to Guillain-Barré syndrome (GBS), a form of neuromuscular paralysis. People suffering from GBS have antibodies to Campylobacter. This makes it a more significant food borne pathogen than previously thought.

Foods most commonly involved in *C. jejuni* outbreaks are meats, poultry, unpasteurized milk, and unchlorinated water. Cross-contamination of foods with raw chicken has been a factor in many of the reported outbreaks. The organism is easily destroyed by most food-processing treatments. Improper use of cutting boards is one of the most-common reasons for an outbreak. Other reasons are poor hygiene and lack of equipment washing. Temperatures of 145°F (63°C) or higher are sufficient to destroy the organism.

Antibiotic treatment with erythromycin is the preferred treatment.

Cholera

Cholera is a bacterial disease that affects the intestinal tract. It is caused by a germ called *Vibno cholera*. People traveling to places where outbreaks are occurring and people who eat undercooked seafood from warm coastal waters subject to sewage contamination are most at risk. The cholera bacteria is passed in the stools. It is spread by eating or drinking water contaminated by the fecal waste of an infected person. This occurs more often in underdeveloped countries lacking adequate water supplies and proper sewage disposal.

People exposed to cholera may experience mild to severe diarrhea, vomiting, and dehydration. Fever is usually absent. The incubation period is six hours to five days after exposure. Because of the rapid dehydration that may result from severe diarrhea, replacement of fluids by mouth or intravenously is critical. Antibiotics, such as tetracycline, are also used to shorten the duration of diarrhea and shedding of the germs in the feces.

A cholera vaccine is available. However, it offers only partial protection (50 percent) for only two to six months.

Cryptosporidiosis

Although cryptosporidiosis is not new, it was not recognized as a cause of human disease until 1976. It is an intestinal illness caused by microscopic parasite called *cryptosporodium*. The most common symptom is diarrhea. It is often accompanied by abdominal cramping, nausea, vomiting, fever, headache, and loss of appetite. Some people infected with cryptosporodium may not become ill.

In healthy individuals with normal immune systems, signs and symptoms generally persist for two weeks or less. However, immuno-compromised people (those with weak immune systems) may have severe and long-lasting illness. These people are receiving cancer chemotherapy, kidney dialysis, steroid therapy, and people with HIV/AIDS and Crohn's disease. The incubation period ranges from one to twelve days, with an average of seven days.

Cryptosporodium is shed in the feces of infected humans and animals.

People become infected by ingesting the organism. Cryptosporodium can be spread from person-to-person or animal-to-person contact and by drinking contaminated water. Infected individuals can shed the organism in their stool for several weeks after they recover from the illness. Because cryptosporidiosis is transmitted by the fecal-oral route, the greatest potential for transmitting the organism comes from infected people who have diarrhea, people with poor personal hygiene, and diapered children.

Some immunity appears to follow infection, but the degree is unclear. No specific treatment for cryptosporidiosis exists, so the treatment is a supportive one for parasites in general.

Dengue hemorrhagic fever

Dengue hemorrhagic fever (DHF) causes a spectrum of illnesses ranging from mild, nonspecific viral syndrome to severe hemorrhagic disease and death. The severe form is called DHF and dengue shock syndrome (DSS). The incubation period on the average is between four to six days.

Denguelike disease has been reported in medical literature as early as 1780. However, it was properly identified during World War II in Asia and the Pacific Theater. The first isolation was made by Japanese health workers. Since that time, thousands of dengue viruses have been isolated.

The symptoms are sudden fever and later hemorrhaging. If the patient is not given fluid replacement, less blood is circulated, leading to shock and death. Dengue fever affects the liver, lungs, kidneys, spleen, lymph nodes, and heart. The most-common hemorrhaging is through the skin, gums, and stomach. Blood plasma must be given.

Dengue viruses are transmitted by mosquitoes, the most important being an urban mosquito, aedes aegypti. The best way to avoid catching a dengue virus is to use insect repellents, such as DEET 2 percent to 3 percent. Dengue viruses are not communicable from person to person, and no quarantine is required. Someone surviving dengue fever is virus free and will have lifetime immunity. However, a survivor may catch other types of dengue fever. There is no cure or vaccine available for this disease. Dengue occurs in most tropical areas of the world. It is found in areas of Asia, the Pacific, and the Americas.

Major epidemics could occur in areas with a lot of mosquitoes. These find ready breeding places in discarded tires where stagnant water accumulates, in poorly maintained urban areas, discarded plastic containers capable of holding water, and areas of poverty with poor sanitation.

Diphtheria

The diphtheria bacteria take up residence in the mouth, throat, and nose of an infected person. It is easily passed to others through coughing or sneezing. Early symptoms are sore throat, a slight fever, and chills. Usually, the disease develops in the throat. It can make it hard to swallow and even cause the patient to suffocate. Some people may be infected, but not appear ill. They can also spread the infection.

If diphtheria is not properly treated, or not treated in time, the bacteria may produce a powerful poison. This poison can spread throughout the body causing serious complications such as heart failure or paralysis. Without treatment, about 10 percent of the people exposed to diphtheria die.

All states have laws requiring vaccination with DTP (diphtheria/tetanus/pertussis). This also protects against tetanus and pertussis. In recent years, a controversy erupted around the subject of vaccination, in particular that associated with diphtheria. The normal side effects of DTP immunization are fever, and local reactions such as redness, pain and swelling are common. Drowsiness, fretfulness, and loss of appetite occur frequently.

There are reports of encephalitis, sudden infant death syndrome (SIDS), transverse myelitis, hyperactivity, learning disorders, and progressive degenerative central nervous system conditions following DTP immunization. The American Academy of Pediatrics, the Child Neurology Society, the Canadian National Advisory Committee on Immunization, the British Joint Committee on Vaccination and Immunization, and the British Pediatric Association all state that such a cause and effect relationship has not been demonstrated, and if it is, then the occurrence of such an event must be exceedingly rare.

The official stance is that the use of the TD vaccine, tetanus toxoid and diphtheria, is safe. Diphtheria during pregnancy may be associated with an increased risk of miscarriage, premature delivery, or harmful effects to the unborn child.

Ebola

The Ebola virus is named after a river in Zaire where it was first discovered. It is a usually fatal filovirus that affects monkeys, apes, and humans, and now thought to affect bats as well. There are other similar viruses, Marburg-Ebola, Ebola Zaire, Ebola Sudan, and Ebola Ruston. Ebola Zaire is 90-percent fatal. Ebola Sudan is 60-percent fatal. The incubation period is seven to fourteen days.

BIOLOGICAL ATTACKS

The virus was first isolated in 1976 at CDC, Porton Down in the United Kingdom and at the Institute for Tropical Diseases in Antwerp, Belgium. It was found to be different from the Marburg virus. Back in 1967 in Marburg, Germany, and in Yugoslavia several workers in a vaccine plant died. They were handling tissues from Ugandan green monkeys, some of which were infected with the virus.

All forms of viral hemorrhagic fevers begin with fever and muscle aches. Then it progresses to vomiting, diarrhea, abdominal pain, respiratory problems, severe bleeding, kidney problems, and shock. Blood fails to clot, and patients bleed from injection sites, the stomach, skin, and internal organs. Even doctors, not known for being squeamish, shudder when they describe it. It is so violent that in Zaire some of the medical staff would not treat the sick, their families had to do it.

Ebola is spread by close personal contact with a person who is very ill. Reuse of hypodermic needles, common in developing countries, is said to have increased the patient load in Zaire. A person is contagious until there is a complete recovery. The Reston, Virginia, strain, first seen in 1989, appears to have been transmitted by air. However, this strain is not harmful to humans. A monkey across the aisle from an infected monkey caught Ebola and died. The reaction was a complete quarantine of the laboratory. Then personnel from CDC, wearing spacesuits, disinfected the place. Much speculation was based upon this incident. Many people wonder what would have happened if the Reston strain was able to infect humans. This is the stuff of nightmares.

Basic treatment for Ebola consists of maintaining fluid levels, both blood and water. After recovery, the person is free of the virus and is not contagious. Two people so far are known to carry antibodies to the virus. All previous outbreaks of Ebola continued only so long as people kept coming in contact with bodily fluids of those infected.

The only good thing one can say about Ebola is that its victims die so quickly that they don't have a chance to spread the infection too far.

A major epidemic is possible because it takes up to two weeks to show symptoms, and people can cover long distances in that time, particularly if they fly. Deficient sanitation and hygiene and decreased immune response due to malnutrition add to the danger of an epidemic. The only good thing one can say about Ebola is that its victims die so quickly that they don't have a chance to spread the infection too far.

There is very little research into finding a vaccine for the Ebola virus, mainly because the fear of an outbreak among the researchers. At present there are only four BL-4 laboratories worldwide with Ebola specimens in deep freeze.

E. coli 0157:H7 infection

E. coli are bacteria that normally live in the intestines of humans and animals. Although most strains of these bacteria are harmless, several are known to produce toxins that can cause diarrhea. One particular *E. coli* strain called 0157:H7 can cause severe diarrhea and kidney damage.

It is acquired by eating food containing the bacteria. It lives in the intestines of some healthy cattle, and contamination of the meat may occur in the slaughtering process. Eating meat that is rare or inadequately cooked is the most common way of getting the infection. Person-to-person transmission may occur if infected people do not wash their hands after using the toilet (it is passed in stools).

People infected with *E. coli* 0157:H7 can develop a range of symptoms. Some may have mild diarrhea or no symptoms at all. Most identified cases develop severe diarrhea and abdominal cramps. Blood is often seen in the stool. Usually little or no fever is present. The incubation period is about three days.

In some people, particularly children under five years of age, the infection can cause a complication called hemolytic uremic syndrome (HUS). This is a serious disease in which red blood cells are destroyed and the kidneys fail. Transfusions of blood or blood-clotting factors as well as kidney dialysis may be necessary. A prolonged hospital stay is often required. Fortunately, most people with HUS recover completely, but it can be fatal.

In Japan the *E. coli* O157 epidemic was a natural by-product of the food distribution system, which is controlled by bureaucrats, trading companies, agribusiness, and a fourth, silent partner, criminal syndicates, or the yakuza. These criminal organizations imported stale or contaminated food products. It is believed that through suspect beef imports that O157 entered the food chain in Japan.

This led to an international scandal as O157 bacteria can survive in a freezer and multiply at temperatures as low as 40°F (4°C) in a meat locker, and therefore, over time, the virulence of bad meat increases. Tracing contaminated meat is not easy because of deregulation. Dozens of Japanese meat packers have invested heavily in feedlots and packing plants in California, Nebraska, and other states. In addition, meat importing involves hundreds of different companies of varying size, from meat suppliers to transportation companies and then onto smaller distributors with yakuza connections.

With this occurrence, we have the world food trade adding to the health threats facing us today. Similarly every year we have recalls of meat products of one type or another due to *E. coli* contamination.

Flesh-eating disease

Flesh-eating disease is the popular name for necrotizing fasciitis, one of the streptococcal bacterial infections. This infection spreads through deep tissues, frequently between muscles. It can occur in several different areas of the body, including the neck. The neck infections are believed to often originate as dental infections. Necrotizing fasciitis is a serious disease. It often progresses rapidly, is difficult to treat, and unfortunately, has a high mortality rate.

The symptoms are red, hot, and swollen skin. Skin may progress to a violet discoloration and blisters form, with necrosis (death) of the subcutaneous tissues. Impeded blood flow may lead to oxygen starvation of the tissues and gangrene. Most severe cases progress within hours, and the death rate is high.

Certain strains of Group A streptococci cause severe infection in susceptible hosts. It usually begins with skin infections at the site of minor wounds or punctures. Early medical treatment is critical. Penicillin is the treatment of choice, along with aggressive surgical removal of infected tissue. Limb amputation may be necessary in advanced cases.

Other streptococcal infections are:

strep throat;

scarlet fever;

rheumatic fever;

rheumatic heart disease;

skin infections;

impetigo;

cellulitis/erysipelas;

bacteremia/sepsis, toxic shocklike syndrome.

Hantavirus

Hemorrhagic fever with renal syndrome (HFRS) has been around for hundreds of years in East Asia. The first Western attention was placed on it during the Korean War. U.S. troops in 1951 came down with hemorrhaging fever. Untreated the mortality rate was 10 percent. Hantavirus pulmonary syndrome (HPS) was identified in 1993 as the cause of the fatal respiratory disease outbreak in the Four Corners region in the U.S. (New Mexico, Arizona, Colorado, and Utah). The mortality rate was 40 to 50 percent. The virus is moving north. April 1997 saw the first fatality in the Canadian province of Ontario.

Hantavirus pulmonary syndrome is characterized by fever, chills, and muscular pain, followed by the abrupt onset of respiratory distress. Death is often from blood leaking from the blood vessels into the air sacs. The symptoms of HFRS are chills, weakness, fatigue, followed by flank pain, nausea and vomiting, diarrhea, headaches, and abdominal pain. The incubation period is eight to forty-two days.

There are many forms. The first was the Sin Nombre virus (SNV, Four Corners virus). Others are named according to where they were found. These are the Seoul, Dobrava-Belgrade, and Puumala viruses. Hantavirus is transmitted from rodent excreta to humans. No insects are involved in transmission. Deer mice are known hosts to HPS.

To avoid hantavirus, one must keep away from wild rodents and their excreta. Make your home rodent proof. There is no vaccine at present. However, work at Fort Detrick and in China is promising. It is endemic in China, Korea, eastern Russia, the Balkans, northern Scandinavia, and the U.S.

Should the rodent population increase in a massive way, a hantavirus epidemic is not just possible, but very likely.

Hepatitis A

Formerly known as infectious hepatitis, hepatitis A is a liver disease caused by a specific virus. It is a fairly common disease. The virus enters through the mouth, multiplies in the body and is passed in the feces. The virus can be carried on an infected person's hand and can be spread by direct contact or by consuming food or drink handled by an infected individual. In some cases, it can be spread by drinking water contaminated with improperly treated sewage.

The symptoms of hepatitis A may include fatigue, poor appetite, fever, and vomiting. Urine may become darker in color, and then jaundice (a yellowing of the skin and whites of the eyes) may appear. The disease is rarely fatal, and most people recover in a few weeks without any complications. The incubation time is between two and six weeks.

Once an individual recovers from hepatitis A, he or she is immune for life and does not continue to carry the virus. There is a vaccine available for hepatitis A.

Hepatitis B

Hepatitis B was formerly known as serum hepatitis. It is a liver disease caused by a virus. Those who share needles, some health-care workers working with blood, homosexual males, hemodyalisis patients, people in the same household with an infected person, and infants born to mothers who are hepatitis B sufferers are most susceptible to hepatitis B.

The symptoms include fatigue, poor appetite, fever, vomiting, occasional joint pain, hives, and rash. Urine may become darker in color, and then jaundice may appear. Some individuals may experience few or no symptoms. The symptoms appear two to six months after exposure. About 10 percent of the infected people may become long-term carriers of the virus. A vaccine is available.

Hepatitis C

Hepatitis C was called non-A, non-B hepatitis. It is a liver disease caused by a recently identified blood-borne virus. Now we even have hepatitis D and E. People who share needles and those receiving blood transfusions are most likely to get hepatitis C.

The symptoms are similar to hepatitis B, however, people with hepatitis C who have jaundice may go on to develop chronic liver disease (50 percent). Information is incomplete at this time.

Influenza

The 1918-19 influenza outbreak killed an estimated twenty-one million people. Its speed in spreading and killing its victims was such that no vaccine could be developed in time. In the late 1990s, we had the "bird flu," and doctors were bracing for an epidemic. Current influenza outbreaks are all originating in China, where ducks and pigs are raised together. An avian virus mutates and jumps to the pigs, which in turn infect humans. Now we have a virus that can infect people directly from chickens. This is why officials in Hong Kong have killed 1.3 million chickens and an untold number of ducks and geese over a minor virus that affected only two dozen people.

The *South China Morning Post* in December 1997 reported on preparations by hospitals to deal with an outbreak of the bird flu. It was reported that the World Health Organization (WHO) hoped to have a vaccine for virus H5N1 by mid-1998. Vaccines of this type are usually prepared by growing the virus in chicken eggs. However, this strain kills the eggs. Now scientists are working on other possible solutions. Professor John Oxford, a leading virologist at the Royal London Hospital Medical School, said, "It's a possibility that the virus is quietly seeding itself and could explode. That's one scenario." He went on to say that proven cases of human-to-human transmission would be really alarming.

The British medical journal, *Lancet*, ran an article on the genetic make-up of H5N1. The article dealt not just with the arrangement of the molecules, but also with its startling clinical features. H5N1's form is different from any other form of influenza in recent memory. Should the avian flu infect anyone already ailing with a human influenza virus, the microbes could exchange genes. This would alter the bird virus to make it easily transmitted from person to person.

The influenza virus constantly changes and seems to keep one step ahead of the fresh vaccines that are prepared each year. Thus the virus can evade antibodies, the proteins that the immune system produces. Given that the three last pandemics started in China, the 1918-19 influenza, the 1956 Asian flu that killed 1,000,000, and the 1968 Hong Kong flu that killed 750,000, we are sure to face additional ones in the future. Another world-wide flu epidemic may place us in a no-win position. In disasters, relief efforts come from staging areas outside the disaster zone. With a world-wide outbreak, everywhere may be a disaster zone, with no staging areas for relief. Relief systems may be overextended and fail.

Mad cow disease

Creutzfeldt-Jacob disease (CJD) and now Variant Creutzfeldt-Jacob (V-CJD) disease became known only through postmortem examination. Bovine spongiform encephalopathy (BSE) is believed to be responsible for mad cow disease. A huge scientific research and discussion is underway to see whether this is the case. This led to a ban on importing British beef and beef products by many countries. In the UK many people stopped eating beef. Since 80 percent of the reported cases of BSE were in dairy cows, many people stopped buying milk from such cows.

The debate is still ongoing on what caused BSE in the first place. Many say that feeding sheep brains to cows is the origin. Scrapie has been in the sheep population for at least two hundred years and has never been known to transmit to humans. And given that farmers as a group had a higher percentage of CJD than the general population, some link between BSE and CJD is assumed.

The symptoms of CJD resemble those of other diseases. Scientists are trying to develop methods of identification and possible cures, but at this time, we do not know enough about this disease.

Malaria

Malaria is a common and serious tropical disease. It is an infection transmitted to human beings by mosquitoes biting mainly between sunset and sunrise. It is a serious problem in more than ninety countries worldwide. References in Assyrian, Chinese, and Indian texts describe an illness that may have been malaria as far back as two thousand years ago. Hippocrates in the fifth century B.C. was the first to describe it in detail. Since close to five hundred million people a year are diagnosed with malaria, mostly in Africa, this is a major health concern.

The symptoms are bouts of fever accompanied with headaches, fatigue, nausea, muscular pains, and light diarrhea. Severe forms have delirium, impaired consciousness, convulsions, followed by persistent coma and death. The incubation period is thirty days. In some strains it may be as long as eight to nine months. Parasites (sporozoite stage) are injected into skin capillaries by a mosquito. From there they travel via the bloodstream to the liver, where they develop and multiply before entering the bloodstream again and invading other organs, including the brain.

In Africa, malaria is described as a disease of utter apathy. The new antimalaria drug, mefloquine, has side effects that consist of vivid, even violent dreams, adding to violence in regions using the drug. A strain of cerebral malaria resistant to mefloquine is now on the increase in sub-Saharan Africa.

Protection from biting mosquitoes is the first line of defense in endemic areas. Removing old tires and other mosquito-breeding grounds help, too. Malaria is a curable disease. Malaria epidemics are likely in refugee movements. We see increased resistance to pesticides by many insects, including mosquitoes.

Plague

Plague is an acute, highly fatal disease caused by infection with Yersinia pestis (older names Bacillus pestis and Pasteurella pestis), a bacterium. The three major clinical forms of the disease are bubonic, septicemic, and pneumonic. Three different types of plague bacteria have been associated with three major pandemics. These biotypes and their associated pandemics are:

antiqua	Justinian's plague
medievalis	black death
orientali	modern pandemic

The first great pandemic was during the reign of Emperor Justinian in 542 A.D. and lasted fifty to sixty years. The regions around the Mediterranean were most affected with a death toll in the tens of millions. The second great pandemic began in 1347 and lasted for four hundred years. Europe, the Middle and Far East suffered casualties of one hundred million or more. The third pandemic broke out in China in the late 1890s. From Chinese ports, it spread worldwide and killed millions.

Typical symptoms of plague are sudden onset of fever, shaking chills, headache, muscle pains, prostration, and stomach upsets. The incubation time is two to six days. (Pneumonic plague can have as little as a one-day incubation.) People with bubonic plague develop infected, swollen, lymph nodes (buboes). These buboes usually occur in the groin, armpits, or areas of the neck. In septicemic plague, the disease enters the bloodstream, and people suffering with it go into septic shock. Pneumonic plague patients have severe pneumonia, shortness of breath, high fever, and often cough up blood.

The lymph nodes are most commonly affected. However, once the plague enters the blood system, it can spread to most organs, including the brain. The infection is transmitted by insects, mostly fleas. Another source is infected animals. The disease can be transmitted by inhalation of infectious respiratory droplets from animals or humans, resulting in primary pneumonic plague.

The basic treatment for all types of plague is antibiotic therapy and quarantine. Recurrence of plague has been rarely reported. Untreated pneumonic plague is almost always fatal. Plague has been reported on all continents but Antarctica. Major new epidemics are possible where rats live in close proximity to humans. Thus rat fleas can readily infect humans. Poverty-stricken areas with poor sanitation are the likely locations.

To illustrate the impact of a wide-scale plague epidemic, we have the writings from 1348 to 1350 detailing the social and economic impacts at that time. Economic chaos, social unrest, high prices, profiteering, depraved morals, lack of production, industrial indolence, frenetic gaiety, wild expenditure, luxury, debauchery, social and religious hysteria, greed, avarice, maladministration, and decay of manners are only a few mentioned. It sounds like today.

BIOLOGICAL ATTACKS

Smallpox (variola major)

A disease believed to have been wiped out twenty years ago is a possible terrorist weapon. Today the remaining cultures are stored in a U.S. research facility and a second one in Russia. There is speculation that Iraq, Israel, China, India, Pakistan, and North Korea have live smallpox viruses in their biological weapon facilities.

The incubation period is twelve to thirteen days. Smallpox begins with fever, malaise, and backache. The rash appears within two to four days and rapidly evolves from a discolored spot on the skin to pimplelike skin eruptions, blisters, and finally crusts. This usually starts on the palms and soles of the feet and feels like shot pellets under the skin. The boils spread across the body. A version called smallpox major is more severe and causes heart failure. The fatality rate for adults is 20 to 60 percent, and most survivors have disfiguring scars.

Smallpox spreads in concentric circles as people have contact with each other. In the case of a smallpox breakout, we would have an unprotected population. The resulting crisis would make the anthrax scare pale in comparison. Smallpox vaccinations ceased in 1973. They are effective for about ten years. Vaccination can't be provided to anyone with immuno suppression, which includes people with HIV, chemotherapy patients, pregnant women, and eczema sufferers.

This is a terror weapon many terrorist organizations would like to have in their arsenals.

Yellow Fever

This is an acute infectious disease and does not last very long. It can range from mild to fatal. There are three forms of it. These are urban, jungle, and sylvan. Yellow fever has been known since the first exploration of Africa. The incubation period is three to six days.

The symptoms are sudden onset of fever, headache, backache, weakness, nausea, and vomiting. This progresses to nosebleeds, fever, bleeding from the mouth, black stools (due to ingested blood), black vomit, and jaundice (which is why it's called yellow fever). It is transmitted by mosquitoes. The three types of yellow fever are based on the type of mosquito vector causing the disease.

Once a person has yellow fever, he can transmit the disease to others. The contagion period lasts from three to five days. Antibiotics have no effect on the yellow fever virus. Support treatment and replacement of lost blood are the current therapies. Yellow fever does not recur in survivors. It is found mostly in Latin America and Africa. Epidemics end when the dry season comes.

Unchecked breeding of mosquitoes and people traveling to get treatment can lead to major epidemics. The natural reservoir for the yellow fever virus is monkeys, with mosquitoes as the transmission vector.

Military uses

"Biological operations is the military employment of living microorganisms to reduce man's ability to wage war. This objective of biological operations may be achieved directly by attacking man and causing disability or death. In addition, it may be achieved indirectly by attacking domestic animals or crops and by that limiting man's sources for food, clothing, and medical supplies. Because warfare or terrorism employing biological agents are antipersonnel rather than antimaterial, housing, buildings, factories, and other structures remain intact and may be used."

The above quote from a military manual sums up very nicely the essence of biological warfare goals. Bruce Sibley, the author of *Surviving Doomsday*, called it "a unique form of madness!" As survivors, we should consider other aspects of survival in a biologically threatening situation. We have the Ebola virus in Zaire, the outbreak of plague in India, and other natural catastrophes that could get out of hand.

Consider a major economic depression coupled with the threat of the spread of a disease against which we have no vaccines. The slowdown of economic activity will delay the development of the vaccine and lack of transportation facilities the distribution of the vaccine. As usual, people in the cities will suffer the most casualties as panic follows. As people flee the cities, the disease will spread with them. Martial law will only be the first step in the government's response to the crisis.

Although biological agents have never been used as significant weapons of war, there is documentary evidence that they have been used in warfare since early times, as mentioned previously.

Because biological warfare has never been experienced on a major scale, no definite evaluation can be made of its effectiveness as a type of warfare. The fact that little is known about the tactical or strategic value of biological agents in modern warfare should not lead to an underestimation of possibilities. It is well established that these agents can now be produced on a scale not considered possible in the past.

A small nation with modern and adequate research facilities could produce biological agents, if only on a small scale. Even the cost of large-scale production would be much less than other weapons of war. Another important consideration is the possibility that new and more-effective methods for mutating organisms will follow from the current work on genes.

Biological agents could be dispersed from a sprayer on a small plane. One flying over Washington, D.C., carrying 100 kilograms (220 pounds) of anthrax spores could deliver a fatal dose to up to three million people. Unlike chemical weapons, which become less potent as they disperse, biological weapons can become more potent, sometimes mutating into even-more toxic forms.

However, a recent scare over the use of crop dusters to distribute biological agents must be tempered by a dose of reality. To modify the crop duster for aerosol spraying of biological materials, changes must be made. Our crop dusters are designed to release chemical through a 100-micron opening (a micron is one millionth of a millimeter). For biological material, they must use a 10-micron opening, resulting in higher pressures for the release mechanism. In addition, the tanks must be thoroughly cleaned. Otherwise the biological agents are deactivated. So the scare was either a red herring or part of a long-range plan.

The recent concern with Iraq's capability to make and use biological weapons is behind the concern of the U.S. and its allied powers. In late 1994, the UN arms-inspection teams discovered documents about Iraq's import of small quantities of medium used to grow bacteria. Later investigation revealed that vast amounts of growth medium had been imported from the British firm of Oxoid. Hospitals use this growth medium in minuscule quantities. Iraq imported 39,000 kilograms in large barrels. The brand of imported growth medium is especially suitable for anthrax or bacillus anthracis. Iraq, of course, denied that the import was for military purposes.

Currently it is probable the biological agents that might be used in warfare would include the following microorganisms: viruses, rickettsias, bacteria, and fungi. Research adds daily to the list of potential biological agents with designer microorganisms. The progress is very rapid to tailor-make an infectious agent for warfare. Gene-manipulation techniques opened a Pandora's box of biological warfare.

The table below shows the well-established biological agents deemed to be suitable for warfare, terrorism, and covert attack on one's enemy. Explanatory notes follow the table.

Potential biological antipersonnel agents

Microorganism	Mode of transmission	Incubation period (days)	Mortality rates (%)	Vaccine	Treatment
Bacteria					
Bacillus antracis (anthrax)	A, D, I	1-7	5-100[1]	+	E[2]
Brucella group (brucellosis)	A, D, I	5-21	2-6	+	E
Francisella tularensis (tularemia)	A, D, I, V	1-10	<30	++	E
Pasteurella pestis (plague)	A, V	2-6	25-100[4]	+++	E[3]
Vibrio comma (Cholera)	I	1-5	15-90	+++	E
Corynebacterium diphtheriae	A, D	2-5	5-12	+++	E
Salmonella typhose (typhoid fever)	I	6-21	7-14	+++	E
Rickettsias					
Rickettsia prowazeki (epidemic or louse-borne typhus)	V	6-15	10-40	+++	E
Rickettsia mooseri (endemic or flea-borne typhus)	V	6-14	2-5	–	E
Rickettsia rickettsii (Rocky Mountain spotted fever)	V	3-10	30	–	E
Coxiella burneti (Q fever)	A, I	14-21	<1	++	E
Viruses					
Group A arboviruses					
Eastern equine encephalitis (EEE)	V[5]	4-24	60	–	N
Venezuelan equine encephalitis (VEE)	V	4-24	–	++	N
Group B arboviruses					
St. Louis encephalitis	V	4-24	–	–	N

Japanese B encephalitis	V	5-15	10-80	++	N
Russian spring-summer encephalitis (RSSE)	V (tick)	7-14	3-40	+	N
Yellow fever	V	3-6	5-40	+++	N
Dengue fever	V	4-10	<1	+	N
Ungrouped arbovirus					
Rift Valley fever	V	4-6	<1	−	N
Poxvirus					
Variola virus (smallpox)	A, D	7-16	1-35	+++	N
Myxovirus					
Rabies virus	A, D[6]	6-365	100	++	E
Fungi					
Coccidivides imitis (coccidioido-mycosis)	A, D	10-21	1-50	−	E
Histoplasma capsulatum (histoplasmosis)	A	5-18	−	−	E

Notes:

Transmission can be by: (A) aerosol, (D) direct contact, (I) ingestion, and (V) vector.

Incubation periods and mortality rates vary according to a number of factors (e.g.: ability of the host to resist infection, infective dose, entranceway, and virulence of the microorganism).

Vaccine: + indicates that vaccine is available but of questionable value, ++ indicates that vaccine is available, but mainly used in high risk individuals, +++ indicates that vaccine is used extensively; − indicates that no vaccine is available.

Treatment: E indicates that effective treatment is available; N indicates no specific treatment.

[1] The 5 percent represents mortality due to skin form; 100 percent represents mortality due to respiratory form.

[2] Treatment must be initiated in the earliest stage of the pulmonary form to be effective.

[3] Same as above.

[4] The 25 percent represents mortality from the bubonic form; 100 percent represents mortality from the pneumonic form.

[5] Mosquitoes are thought to be the primary vectors for most viruses.

[6] Direct contact refers to being bitten by a rabid animal, which is the usual means of transmission or coming into contact with a rabid animal.

Toxins, which are the poisonous products of microorganisms, plants and animals, are considered to be chemical agents and will be considered in the next chapter.

Viruses

All viruses are parasitic microorganisms that live in the cells of their selected hosts. Viruses are so small that they will pass through filters that stop bacteria and rickettsias. In addition, they cannot be seen through even the most powerful optical microscopes. They range in size from about 0.01 to 0.27 microns across their greatest dimension.

Viruses are composed of ribonucleic acid (RNA) and a protein coat. They do not contain most of the components found in an ordinary cell. Strangely, once a virus enters a living cell, it is capable of taking over the metabolic processes of the invaded cell. Thus, the virus persuades the host cell to manufacture virus protein and RNA or DNA rather than cell constituents required by the host. It is doubtful that all viruses are essentially of the same nature. The very small forms like the crystalline mosaic viruses of tobacco and cucumbers might be inanimate, while the larger ones are among the smallest microorganisms.

> *Diseases of viral origin do not respond to treatment with antibiotics.*

Virus induced diseases–Viruses are responsible for many important diseases of man, animals, and plants. Human diseases caused by viruses include poliomyelitis, rabies, smallpox, yellow fever, encephalitis, mumps, measles, chickenpox, influenza, and the common cold. Important animal diseases caused by viruses are rinderpest and foot-and-mouth disease in cattle, hog cholera and African swine fever (similar to hog cholera but more acute), distemper and rabies in dogs, fowl disease and Newcastle disease in poultry. Typical viral infections in plants are tobacco and cucumber mosaic diseases and curly-top disease in sugar beets.

Cell response to viruses–Cells infected with viruses shows the following responses: degeneration and death, transformation to a neoplastic state, or survival without transformation, but with evidence of the presence of one or more viral components. Diseases of viral origin do not respond to treatment with antibiotics. Viruses have primary military potential as antipersonnel agents.

Rickettsias–They are intracellular, parasitic microorganisms considered intermediate in size between bacteria and viruses. They are from 0.3 to 0.5 microns in length and about 0.3 microns in diameter. Rickettsias resemble viruses in their strict growth requirements for living host cells. They are usually removed by bacterial filters and are gram-negative (do not hold the purple dye when treated by Gram's method), nonmotile, and nonsporulating. They are easily killed by heat, dehydration, or disinfectants. Studies with an electron microscope show a homogeneous or slightly granular interior structure resembling that of bacteria.

Most rickettsias are parasites, primarily of lower animals and anthropoids. They are transmitted to man and animals by such vectors as ticks, lice, fleas, and mites. There are no known rickettsial diseases in plants. The rickettsias not only require living tissue for reproduction, they have a selective affinity for specific types of cells of the human and animal body.

> **Rickettsias-induced diseases**—Human diseases caused by rickettsias include typhus fever, spotted fever, scrub typhus, and Q fever. An animal disease caused by rickettsias is known as "heartwater" or veldt disease, which is fatal to cattle, sheep, and goats in South Africa. Rickettsias have a primary military potential as antipersonnel agents.

Bacteria—Bacteria are single-celled, microscopic, plantlike organisms. It is estimated that bacteria comprise 60 to 65 percent of microorganisms. Bacteria occur nearly everywhere in nature, but most are harmless, and many are even beneficial to man. Of approximately two thousand identified species, only about one hundred are known to be pathogenic. While most bacteria that infect man are selective human parasites, some are primarily parasites of lower animals that are occasionally transmitted to man.

A typical bacterial cell can be divided into four main subdivisions: the cell wall, cytoplasmic membrane, cytoplasm, and chromatin body. Additional structures that bacteria might possess include flagella for movement, fimbriae (filamentous appendages) that function as organs of attachment, and capsules (a viscous layer covering the cell) that provide a protective coat, store food, act as a site for waste disposal, and in some cases, increase the pathogenicity of certain pathogens.

Classification by shape—Although bacteria are somewhat variable in form, they may be classified according to shape into three main groups:

Bacilli (singular bacillus). Rod shaped.

Cocci (singular coccus). Round or spherical. The cocci are then further classified into groups based on the manner in which they cling together after cell division.

Spirilla (singular spirillum). Comma shaped or spiral. The spirilla are further designated according to specific shape.

Bacteria-induced diseases–Bacteria cause many common diseases of man, animals, and plants. Representative of the coccal (round) forms are the staphylococci, some of which cause boils and food poisoning and the streptococcal sore throat. The gonococci cause gonorrhea, and the meningococci cause one form of meningitis. Representatives of the bacilli (rod-shaped) cause tuberculosis, anthrax, typhoid fever, bacillary dysentery, bubonic plague, brucellosis (undulant fever), and glanders.

Cholera is caused by a comma-shaped vibrio and syphilis by a spiral or corkscrew-shaped spirochete. Diphtheria, tetanus, gas gangrene, and botulism are caused principally by the toxins produced by bacillary organisms. Among diseases of plants caused by bacteria is the bacterial wilt of corn and "soft rot" of vegetables. Bacteria have primary military potential as antipersonnel agents.

Fungi–Fungi are unicellular or multicellular members of the plant kingdom. They include molds, mildews, smuts, rusts, mushrooms, toadstools, puffballs, and yeasts. The cells of most fungi are larger than those of bacteria and range from three to fifty microns in size. They are usually rod-shaped and arranged end to end in strands or filaments.

Fungi diseases affecting man–While fungi produce many serious plant diseases, relatively few important diseases of man or animals are caused by this group of organisms. Fungal diseases in man are for the most part low-grade chronic infections such as ringworm and "athlete's foot." Some fungi, however, are capable of producing serious diseases, examples of which are histoplasmosis and coccidioidomycosis.

Histoplasmosis is characterized by benign involvement of lymph nodes of the trachea and bronchi or by a severe, progressive, generalized involvement of the lymph nodes and the reticuloendothelial system (comprising all the phagocytic cells of the body except the circulating leukocytes). Although the progressive form of this disease is usually fatal, less than one percent of the naturally occurring primary infections develop into the progressive form.

Coccidioidomycosis is characterized by fever and localized pulmonary symptoms. There is a secondary, progressive form of the disease that involves all organs of the body, including the skin and bones, and is often fatal.

Other less-threatening fungal diseases of man are favus, cryptococcosis, thrush, blastomycosis, and sporotrichosis.

Fungus diseases affecting plants–Fungi produce many serious diseases in plants, such as brown spot in rice and rice blast; late blight of potato; cereal rusts; southern blight of sugar beets, white potatoes, and other root crops; smuts; ergot on rye grain; and many others. Fungi have military potential primarily as antiplant agents.

Distribution of biological agents–If antipersonnel biological agents are to be effective in producing disease, they must be distributed in ways that will allow them to enter the body at specific places. These paths include the skin, eyes, mouth, respiratory tract, digestive tract, and genitourinary tract. Our natural body defenses usually are capable of overcoming even large numbers of some invading microorganisms provided they are confined to certain tissues of the body. On the other hand, the natural body defenses frequently may be overwhelmed by just a few of these microorganisms if they gain entrance into certain other organs or tissues.

For example, a large number of intestinal microorganisms (*Escherichia coli*) are normally present in the intestines without causing any disease symptoms. However, only a few of these same organisms in the genitourinary tract can cause a serious infection of the bladder or kidneys.

If invading pathogens enter the body through "unusual" pathways, resulting disease symptoms may be difficult to diagnose. Moreover, mortality rates may be increased.

Three effective methods for distributing antipersonnel biological agents are:

1. the aerosol respiratory method;
2. the anthropoid vector cutaneous method;
3. the covert (sabotage) method.

Related procedures may be used to distribute antianimal and antiplant biological agents.

Aerosol Respiratory Method–An aerosol consists of finely divided particles, either liquid or solid, suspended in a gaseous medium. A biological agent aerosol is an airborne suspension of particles containing living pathogenic organisms.

Its use allows widespread, penetrating coverage, which in field concentrations cannot be detected by the physical senses. For the biological agent aerosol to be effective when inhaled by target personnel, the microorganisms must be viable and virulent (capable of invasiveness and toxicity). These also must be in a particle size that can enter the respiratory tract and be retained in the deep portions of the lungs.

The natural defensive features of the upper respiratory tract, such as the mucous membranes, shell-type compartments within the nose, and cilia of the trachea and bronchial tree, are capable of trapping most particles smaller than one micron and are usually exhaled from the lungs before they have time to settle. Therefore particles in the size range from one to five microns are much-more capable of passing through the defensive barriers of the upper respiratory tract and of being retained in the lungs than those below or above this size range.

Ultraviolet light in sunlight can kill most pathogens relatively quickly. Distribution of an aerosol during the hours of darkness eliminates effects of ultraviolet radiation. Subfreezing temperatures that freeze the biological aerosols tend to preserve the agent and decrease its rate of decay.

Anthropoid vector cutaneous method–A second method for distributing biological agents involves anthropoid vectors (carriers). These anthropoid vectors include mosquitoes, flies, fleas, lice, ticks, and mites. They are capable of transferring pathogens to man by penetrating the skin as they bite.

Athropoid vectors have characteristics that can be used in military situations.

1. The ability to penetrate skin makes circumvention of the protective mask possible.

2. The normal life span of an anthropoid vector is related to the persistency of the agent in the target area. Persistency may be one to two months for some mosquitoes, and six to seven months for some fleas. A few of the ticks are able to pass the agent from generation to generation.

3. The agent inside the body of the vector is protected from external environmental effects for the life of the vector.

4. Female mosquitoes, requiring a warm-blood meal before egg production, search for a warm-blood source by infil-

trating caves, entrenchments, and underground fortifica-
tions inhabited by personnel.

Covert (sabotage) method—Biological agents lend themselves well to covert action because of varying incubation periods, detection difficulties, the variety of agents that could be employed, the ways of employing biological agents, and the minute quantities of agents needed to cause disease. The primary target in covert action may be the respiratory tract; the second target may be the digestive tract. The saboteur or terrorist might employ a small quantity of a biological antipersonnel agent aerosol when his target is the respiratory tract. He might contaminate food and water with pathogens when his target is the digestive tract.

Treatment of casualties—Casualties of biological agents will not require emergency treatment similar to the urgent treatment that is necessary for nerve agent casualties. The treatment of casualties who have contracted a disease as a result of exposure to a biological agent will not differ appreciably from the treatment of those who contact the disease naturally. Once the agent employed in a biological attack has been identified, a plan of action for treatment can be initiated. Such a plan might include antimicrobial drugs for prophylaxis (prevention) and/or therapy, supportive care, and passive immunization.

Preattack—Prior to a biological attack, very great emphases should be placed on personal hygiene, immunization, and sanitation. Good personal hygiene tends to improve the general health of the individual. Since the infective dose is partly dependent upon the condition of the exposed individual, a healthy person is less likely to contract the disease. In many cases, disease symptoms will be less severe or even absent in those who have been immunized.

During attack—During a biological attack, providing that there's warning, the most important item of protective equipment is a properly fitted protective mask in good operating condition. Ordinary clothing, arranged to cover as much of the skin area as possible, will give good protection against field concentrations of biological agents. However, any open wounds should be bandaged.

Postattack—After a biological attack, a primary objective should be decontamination of personnel, equipment, food, and water.

Biological Agent Detection

Currently, no equipment is available for field issue to detect biological agents in time for personnel to take protective action, such as donning protective masks. Additional factors contributing to the difficulty in detecting biological agents after an attack are:

1. Pathogenic microorganisms are invisible to the unaided eye, and they do not exhibit characteristic colors or odors.

2. The interval between exposure to biological agents and the onset of apparent effects may be a matter of days rather than seconds or hours, as is the case with chemical agents.

3. Individuals exposed to the same dosage of a biological agent may not be affected to the same degree. Consequently, it is probable that a well-executed biological attack will not be recognized at the time it occurs and that resultant disease in personnel initially will be indistinguishable from a natural epidemic.

Indications of a biological attack are the following:

1. enemy aircraft dropping unidentified material or spraying unidentified substances;

2. new and unusual types of shells and bombs, particularly those that burst with little or no blast;

3. smokes and mists of unknown source or nature;

4. unusual substances on the ground or on vegetation and any unexplained containers, such as glass bottles or other breakable containers lying around;

5. an increased occurrence of sick or dead animals such as dogs, livestock, or birds;

6. unusual or unexplained increase in the number of insects, such as mosquitoes, ticks, or fleas;

7. any weapon not seeming to have any immediate casualty effect;

8. any food or water suspected of making you ill.

Decontamination

Currently, no standard field or automatic biological agent detection devices are available. Therefore, a rapid determination of biological contamination cannot be made. Safety precautions must be taken not only against the harmful effects of pathogenic agents, but also against the damaging effects of specific decontamination.

The major classes of decontaminants, both natural and chemical are:

Weather—Killing microorganisms through dehydration and exposure to sunlight is the principal means by which weather accomplishes biological decontamination. Since weathering is the simplest method of biological decontamination, it should be used whenever possible.

Elements of weather that can affect biological decontamination include low humidity, sunlight, and rain. Many microorganisms are dried out (dehydrated) when the moisture content in the air is low. Direct exposure to ultraviolet and infrared radiation in sunlight will kill most biological agents within one day. However, biological spores being resistant to adverse conditions can survive low humidity and direct exposure to sunlight for a long time. Rainfall tends to wash many microorganisms out of the air and off objects within an area. The wetting of the terrain may prevent the formation of secondary aerosols and may cause leaching of the organisms into the soil.

Water—Washing or flushing a contaminated area with water serves to remove much of the biological agent. The effectiveness of this procedure is increased when high water pressure is used, contact time is extended, temperature of the water is elevated, soaps or detergent are added to the water, the surface is scrubbed, or when live steam is used in flushing the surface. Water used for decontamination becomes contaminated and should be carefully controlled.

Burial or heat—In special situations, such as those resulting from spillage of an agent or the disposal of bulk agents and waste, decontamination may be accomplished by burying the contaminated material beneath the earth or by using fire. Appropriate items of equipment may be decontaminated by dry heat in an oven of 170°C (335°F) for two to three hours.

Chemical decontaminants–Many of the chemical decontaminants and procedures used in the decontamination of chemical agents are also effective for biological agents. Among these decontaminants is STB (super tropical bleach), STB slurry, DS2, and caustic soda. However, it should be noted that DS2 is not effective against bacterial spores. Moreover, while STB can be used in dry form for biological decontamination, it is more effective when applied as a slurry because chlorine is released faster. In wet form, STB suppresses secondary aerosols.

Formaldehyde solution (formalin) and methyl alcohol (methanol)–Formaldehyde solution is a clear, colorless liquid with a suffocating, pungent odor. This decontaminant may be used either alone or mixed with methanol. A recommended mixture consists of 36 to 40 percent by weight of formaldehyde gas in an aqueous methanol solvent. Formaldehyde solution, separately or in a mixture with methanol, is an effective interior biological decontaminant and may be used when BPL (beta-propiolactone) is not available.

Personnel exposed to formalin vapor should wear a protective mask and washable outer clothing, such as coveralls, fastened at the wrists, ankles, and neck to prevent vapor entering. Rubber boots are preferable to leather. Immediately after emerging from formalin vapor, personnel should remove outer clothing. Moreover, personnel who are exposed to formalin for more than a few minutes should wear self-contained breathing apparatus. Exposure time for decontamination in a closed structure should be sixteen hours.

After decontamination, aeration up to seventy-two hours may be necessary before it is safe to reenter a building. Formalin vapor leaves a deposit of an almost insoluble, toxic, white powder that can be removed only with difficulty by washing with hot water. Using a methanol mixture decreases the extent of residue left, reduces the needed exposure time by about one-half, and decreases the time required for aeration.

Formalin vapor is not a good decontaminant for closed books and tightly packed papers. Valuable papers and records should be removed before decontamination because formalin tends to curl and discolor them.

Decontaminating agent, ethylene oxide–The military issues this in twelve-ounce dispensers as aerosol type M-10. This decontaminating agent is a nonflammable mixture containing 12-percent ethylene oxide (ETO) and 88-percent fluorinated hydrocarbons. It is one of the best biological decontaminants for equipment because it penetrates into remote crevices and recesses. Because ETO vapor is noncorrosive on metals, it may be used safely on delicate electronic equipment. It may also be used on books, papers, leather, fabrics, and clothing. However, care must be exercised to prevent the liquid as it emerges from the dispenser from collecting on the materials being decontaminated since the liquid is harmful to some materials.

A protective mask or other respiratory device and rubber gloves should be worn when using the ETO-fluorinated hydrocarbon mixture. The fumes of ETO are toxic and should not be inhaled. The first warning of the presence of ETO fumes is a sweetish odor followed by the irritation of the eyes and nose. If liquid ETO gets on the skin, it may be removed by blotting with a dry cloth. The skin must be kept uncovered to allow complete evaporation. Clothing or shoes that are wet with ETO must be removed immediately and should not be worn until they are completely dry and aerated. Items that are worn next to the skin should be aerated at least eighteen hours to prevent blistering of the skin.

Vapors of ETO mixture may be used to decontaminate small items in a plastic (polyethylene) bag. One twelve-ounce dispenser should be adequate to decontaminate one set of clothing or one batch of small equipment. Large equipment such as vehicles may be decontaminated with vapors of this mixture under tarpaulin. Enclosures must be airtight for this decontaminant to be effective. At 21° to 26°C (70° to 80°F), the contact time should be from six to eight hours. For each 18°F increase from 80°F, the exposure time can be halved. The decontaminant should not be used below 15°C (60°F). A high humidity is not required.

Sodium hypochlorite (household bleach)—Sodium hypochlorite is a good biological decontaminant. Commercial brands of household bleach contain about 5.25 percent available chlorine and can be applied full strength to decontaminate small areas of terrain and small pieces of equipment. Household bleach should be diluted (one half cup of bleach to one gallon of water) for the decontamination of cotton clothing and utensils. Cotton clothing should be immersed in the bleach solution for thirty minutes and then thoroughly rinsed in clear water to prevent deterioration. This decontaminant is not recommended for woolen items.

Peracetic acid (PAA)—Peracetic acid is a highly efficient decontaminant for biological agents. It is obtained as a 40-percent solution and is diluted to a 2-percent solution for use in biological decontamination. PAA should be diluted with water immediately before use because it gradually decomposes to form hydrogen peroxide and acetic acid. The 40-percent solution should be stored in the original container and refrigerated to reduce the decomposition loss to less than 0.1 percent per month.

While occasional contact with 2-percent PAA solution has little harmful effect on the skin, 40-percent PAA solution on the skin will burn and blister unless immediately washed off with water. Moreover, the 40-percent solution is toxic and must be handled with care. It has a very low flash point of $40^{\circ}C$ ($104^{\circ}F$), and it must be kept away from an open flame. If fire occurs, it can be extinguished with water. Contamination with heavy metal ions may result in an explosion. PAA fumes are very irritating to the mucous membranes of the nose and throat and should be avoided. Personnel preparing and using PAA solution should wear protective masks and rubber gloves.

Prolonged exposure to a 2-percent PAA solution will cause corrosion of iron and deterioration of rubber, plastics, and leather. However, glass, aluminum, stainless steel, plastics, and rubber are not affected by an exposure time sufficient to accomplish decontamination. The protective mask may be wiped with a 2-percent PAA solution without visible damage to the rubber portions or the head harness. Cotton-tipped swabs may be used to apply PAA to crevices that are difficult to reach. Immerse small items in the solution for ten to fifteen minutes or until there is no longer an objectionable odor. A 2-percent solution is compatible with detergents.

Decontamination procedures–During biological operations, individuals should habitually and as frequently as possible scrub the body thoroughly with soap or detergent and hot water and change to clean clothing. Contaminated clothing should be washed thoroughly with hot soapy water and boiled if possible. Protective masks should be decontaminated when feasible. Any minor cuts and abrasions should be treated by ordinary first-aid measures.

If personnel are exposed to biological contamination, a thorough rubdown with 70-percent ethyl alcohol or 80-percent isopropyl alcohol is recommended. All parts of the body should be treated with the alcohol, being especially careful around the eyes.

BIOLOGICAL ATTACKS

Biological agent decontamination methods

Item	Method	Remarks
Clothing: Cotton	Boil in water for 15 minutes **or** autoclave for 45 minutes at 123°C (253°F) **or** immerse in 2% household bleach solution for 30 minutes, rinse immediately **or** launder **or** use vapors of ETO-fluorinated hydrocarbon mixture in plastic (polyethylene) bag–use one 12-ounce dispenser for one set of clothing. Leave clothing in bag for 8 hours, then aerate 1 hour.	Destroys or inactivates all but highly resistant spores. Aerate items that are to be worn next to the skin to prevent blistering for at least 18 hours.
Wool	Use ETO vapors as above **or** launder.	As above.
Protective mask, faceplate and carrier	Wash in warm soapy water, rinse in clear water, and dry at room temperature **or** use ETO vapors as above then wash to remove vapors **or** wipe with 2% peracetic acid, wipe off excess immediately, and aerate 15 minutes.	Aerate items that are to be worn next to the skin for at least 18 hours.
Fine Instruments	Use ETO vapors, then aerate one hour.	
Helmets and mess gear	Use ETO vapors, then aerate a few minutes **or** wash with soap and water, then immerse in disinfectant solution **or** boil in water for 15 minutes **or** immerse in 2% household bleach solution, and rinse **or** immerse in 2% peracetic acid for 10 minutes, rinse, and aerate 15 minutes.	
Leather and rubber items	Use ETO vapors and aerate for 16 hours before wearing **or** immerse in 2% household bleach solution **or** wipe with 2% peracetic acid, remove excess, and aerate 15 minutes. Immerse small items for 10 minutes, and aerate for 15 minutes.	Scrub with hot soapy water before using the vapor method.

Weapons	Use calcium hypochlorite, household bleach solution **or** soap and water.	Dry and lubricate working parts and surfaces afterward.
Vehicles in open	Apply calcium hypochlorite. Leave on 30 minutes, then remove by washing with a stream of water **or** wash with detergent and high-pressure water stream **or** steam clean using detergent.	
Vehicles in airtight shelters or in warm weather under a tarpaulin	Use four 12-ounce dispensers of ETO-fluorinated hydrocarbon mixture for each 100 cubic feet at 75°F and 70% relative humidity, with a contact time of 6 hours or use vapors of BPL (beta-propiolactone) **or** formalin if ETO mixture is not available.	Cover wet ground with tarpaulin before vehicles are set in place.
Buildings, exterior	Apply hypochlorite. Leave on at least 30 minutes, then flush with water **or** apply STB slurry to vertical surfaces by manual means. Slurry may be left on exteriors. Leave it to the weather.	Sun and rain eliminate most microorganisms within 1 day.
Buildings, interior	Fumigate with formalin and steam. Spray approx. 1 ml of formalin per cubic foot **or** wash with soap and water.	Seal building before fumigation, and aerate thoroughly afterward.
Air (in inhabited enclosed spaces)	Filter air by means of a protective collector.	Renders air relatively free from microorganisms.
All types of terrain.	Weather	Evacuate contaminated area or remain masked, and allow sufficient time for weathering.
Porous ground	Wet with water **or** apply 2% household bleach solution **or** apply slurry of 7 parts STB and 93 parts water (by weight) **or** apply caustic soda.	
Hard-surfaced roads	Pour, spray or spread oil.	Will help prevent secondary aerosols.

| Water | Boil small amounts 15 minutes **or** chlorinate **or** add iodine purification tablets to small amounts of water **or** use chlorination kit (Lyster bag). | |
| Food | Food directly exposed should be boiled in water 15 minutes. Cook thoroughly. Canned food or sealed pouches should be immersed in or sprayed with 2% household bleach solution or use ETO vapors. | Thorough cooking ensures destruction of microorganisms. |

Why did we spend so much time on bugs? Because as William H. McNeill wrote in *Plagues and People* (1976), "Ingenuity, knowledge, and organization alter but cannot cancel humanity's vulnerability to invasion by parasitic forms of life. Infectious disease which antedated the emergence of humankind will last as long as humanity itself, and will surely remain, as it has been hitherto, one of the fundamental parameters and determinants of human history."

Under conditions of turmoil, cut off from medical facilities we will be as helpless as our cavemen ancestors. Yup, our future will largely be determined by microbes we can only see under a microscope and sometimes not even then.

7
CHEMICAL ATTACKS

"Chemical agents can be used both tactically and strategically in either a nuclear or a nonnuclear environment within the range of weapons and aircraft. They can be used to provide concealment, to damage material, to start fires, to injure animals, and to poison food, water, grain or forage. However, chemical agents are used primarily to inflict casualties or to harass personnel. They are also used to contaminate strategic areas and to make these areas impassable or untenable. Furthermore, chemical agents tend to demoralize personnel and by that reduce their military efficiency."

The above quotation was taken from an older U.S. Navy handbook on nuclear, biological, and chemical (NBC) warfare. To the quotation, we can add the use of chemical weapons by insurgents, terrorists, and the like. Thus we have a terror weapon aimed against mostly civilian or unprepared targets. Note the effect of sarin used in the Tokyo subway system. It resulted in near paralysis for much of that city's transport network.

The use of chemical weapons is not a recent event. Ancient Greek city-states overwhelmed opponents with the noxious fumes of smoldering pitch and sulphur. Chinese warriors wafted arsenic-laced smoke screens against their foes. On April 22, 1915, German troops twisted open the valves on five thousand canisters of chlorine gas at Ypres, Belgium, and massive green clouds made their way toward allied forces. Within minutes, thousands of panicked victims died.

Chemical warfare was used in the Vietnam War in the guise of Agent Orange and other defoliants. The goal was to deny cover to the Viet Cong and North Vietnamese forces. Herbicides have been developed to eliminate coca plantations.

Types of Chemical Agents

Nerve agents–Nerve agents are quick acting, casualty-producing chemical agents that cause an imbalance between the sympathetic and parasympathetic nervous systems. This imbalance results in the continual stimulation of the nervous system and characteristic physiological symptoms. Death is caused by anoxia (oxygen deficiency) due to respiratory failure, from weakness of the respiration muscles, depression of the central nervous system, and airway obstruction by bronchial and salivary secretions.

G-agents and V-agents–Currently there are two series or groups of nerve agents: the G-series and the V-series. The G-series is composed of Tabun (GA), sarin (GB), and soman (GD). The standard V-agent is VX.

The physical properties of the G-agents are similar. GA is a colorless to brownish liquid giving a colorless vapor. It has a faintly fruity odor when impure, none when pure. GB and GD are colorless to light brown liquids giving colorless vapors. While GB has almost no odor in the pure state, GD has a fruity odor when in the pure state and has the odor of camphor when impure. Although all three G-agents are comparatively volatile liquids, GB is more volatile than either GA or GD.

V-agents are colorless and odorless liquids. They are less volatile than the G-agents and are consequently more persistent. It is of practical importance that V-agents are absorbed by the vegetation. VX will last sixteen weeks in winter, three weeks in summer, but only twelve hours in rain.

Sarin (isopropyl methylphosphonofluoridate) is one of the nerve gases invented by the Germans, who were searching for superior pesticides. It can be synthesized from direct conversion of phosphorus trichloride into methylphosphonic dichloride. The process was published some years ago in the *Canadian Journal of Chemistry*. A qualified chemist or a specialized chemical technician can handle the synthesization. Another route starting with elemental phosphorus and chlorine is also possible if the intermediate materials are not available. Until such time as Russia offers employment opportunities to former chemical warfare workers they can be hired by any group with money.

Nerve gas exposure results in symptoms ranging from a runny nose and blurred vision to cessation of breathing and death. These symptoms occur within thirty seconds if the exposure dose is large enough, but more likely doses would take one to ten minutes to cause death.

V-agents that enter the body by inhalation are about five times as toxic as G-agents. V-agents that enter the body through the skin are several hundred times more toxic than G-agents. If VX enters via the mouth, the first symptom is intestinal cramping.

Nerve agents can be dispersed by artillery shell, mortar shell, missile, bomb, aircraft spray, or land mine.

Blister agents poison food and water and make other supplies dangerous to handle.

Blister Agents (vesicants)–Blister agents are used for casualty effect and they may produce long-term incapacitation or even death. These agents act on the eyes, lungs, and skin. They burn and blister the skin or any other part of the body they touch. They damage the respiratory tract when inhaled and cause vomiting and diarrhea when absorbed. Furthermore, blister agents poison food and water and make other supplies dangerous to handle.

Types of blister agents–These are Lewinstein mustard (H), distilled mustard (HB), nitrogen mustard (HN), lewisite (L), other arsenicals, mixtures of mustards and arsenicals, and phosgene oxime (CX). These are persistent gases and will last up to eight weeks in the winter, seven days in the summer, and only two days through a rainy period.

Lewinstein mustard (H), which is made by the Lewinstein process, contains about 30-percent sulfur impurities, which give it a pronounced odor. HD is H that has been purified by washing and vacuum distillation. HD has less odor, a slightly greater blistering power (negligible in the field), and more stability in storage than H. In general the properties of H are essentially the same as for HD. Both H and HD have garliclike or horseradishlike odors. At 20°C (room temperature) and normal atmospheric pressure, distilled mustard (HD) is an oily liquid ranging from colorless when pure to dark brown when production plant run.

Although mustard is heavier than water, small droplets float on water surfaces and thus represent a special hazard in contaminated areas. Mustard is only slightly soluble in water, which gradually destroys it, but undissolved mustard may persist in water for long periods. It is most soluble in fats and oils. It is freely soluble in gasoline, kerosene, acetone, carbon tetrachloride, and alcohol. These solvents do not destroy mustard. Mustard disappears from contaminated ground or materials through evaporation or hydrolysis. It can be destroyed rapidly by using decontaminating chemicals or by boiling in water.

Neither mustard vapor nor liquid produces any immediate symptoms. Generally symptoms appear four to six hours later, when the eyes begin to smart, the skin becomes red and blistered, and the victim coughs and vomits. The rate of detoxification is very low, which means that even very small repeated exposures are cumulative in their effect. The duration of the effectiveness of mustard depends upon both the munitions used and the weather. Heavily splashed liquid persists one to two days under average weather conditions and a week or more under very cold conditions.

The nitrogen mustards are a group of related compounds that may be considered derivatives of ammonia (NH_3) because the hydrogen atoms are replaced by various organic radicals. Three members of the group are HN-1, HN-2, and HN-3. At 20°C and normal atmospheric pressure, the nitrogen mustards are oily, colorless, or pale-yellow liquids that are somewhat soluble in water, but easily soluble in organic solvents. HN-1 has a fishy or musty odor; HN-2 has a soapy odor in low concentrations and a fruity odor in high concentrations; HN-3, if pure, has no odor. While HN-2 is rated as somewhat more toxic than HN-1, HN-3 is regarded as the most toxic of the nitrogen mustards. Detoxification does not occur, and the effects are cumulative.

Because HN-2 is highly unstable, it is no longer considered as a chemical agent. HN-1 is more volatile and less persistent than HD, but it is only one-fifth as vesicant to the skin as HD. HN-3 is less volatile and more persistent than HD and has about equal vesicancy. Because HN-3 is the most stable in storage of the three nitrogen mustards, it is considered well suited for artillery shells. The nitrogen mustards are less readily hydrolyzed than mustard, and all their hydrolytic products, except the final ones, are toxic.

At 20°C and normal atmospheric pressure, all arsenical vesicants are colorless to brown liquids. They are soluble in most organic solvents, but are poorly soluble in water. In general, arsenical vesicants are more volatile than mustard (HD) and have fruity to geraniumlike odors. These vesicants react rapidly with water to yield the corresponding solid arsinoxides, with concurrent loss of volatility and most of their vesicant properties. Liquid arsenical vesicants gradually penetrate rubber and most impermeable fabrics.

Lewisite (L) is one of the most important of the arsenical vesicants. At normal temperature and pressure, lewisite is a dark oily liquid, which generally has a geraniumlike odor although it has very little odor when pure. The rate of action on personnel is rapid. Even though the body exposed to lewisite does not detoxify, detoxification can be induced through intramuscular injection of BAL in oil. The duration of effectiveness of L is somewhat shorter than the duration of the effectiveness of HD.

Arsenical vesicants such as lewisite (L) are often mixed with mustard. Although these mixtures do not produce more-severe lesions than either agent alone, they tend to confuse and make diagnosis difficult. A mustard-lewisite mixture is generally a variable mixture of HD and L that provides a low-freezing mixture for use in cold-weather operations or as a high-altitude spray. The eutectic mixture, which is the mixture having the lowest possible freezing point, is 63 percent L and 37 percent HD by weight. Other mixtures such as fifty-fifty may be prepared to meet predetermined weather conditions and have advantages over the eutectic mixture because of the increased HD content.

Mixtures of H and L are unsatisfactory because of poor storage characteristics. At normal temperature and pressure, mustard-lewisite mixtures are dark, oily liquids that have a garlicky odor. The body does not detoxify these mixtures. How long mustard-lewisite mixtures are effective depends on the munitions used and the weather. The duration is somewhat shorter than the duration of effectiveness of HD.

Phosgene oxime (CX) is an example of a class of chemical agents called urticant or nettle gases. While these agents are primarily irritants to the skin and mucous surfaces, they differ from mustard by producing an immediate sensation of pain. This pain may vary from mild prickling to something akin to a severe bee sting. CX may appear as a liquid or as a colorless, low-melting-point (crystalline) solid that is readily soluble in water. It has a high vapor pressure and slowly decomposes at normal temperatures (depending on temperature and humidity). CX boils at 53-54°C (28 mm of pressure) and melts at 39-40°C. Phosgene oxime is a powerful irritant, and it's especially effective as a liquid.

Protective clothing–A mask and permeable clothing can provide some protection against vesicant vapors. However, personnel should wear impermeable protective clothing for protection against liquid vesicants.

All nerve agents can enter the body through inhalation, ingestion, or absorption through the skin and eyes. Therefore a mask alone does not offer adequate protection against these agents.

Ordinary clothing affords no special protection against any nerve agents, and moreover, ordinary clothing exposed to nerve agent vapors may give off these vapors for an appreciable time after the exposure. This fact should be considered before unmasking. All liquid nerve agent contamination on ordinary clothing should be removed immediately.

> *The Gulf War brought out the shortcomings of all present masks and protective clothing. Had Iraq used chemical weapons, the casualties would have been very high.*

Permeable protective clothing provides only very limited protection against V-agents and even-less protection against G-agents. This type of clothing does not protect against large drops or splashes of nerve agents. Even small droplets will penetrate clothing after several hours.

The only protection is by wearing nonpermeable protective clothing. These are specially designed to protect against all known chemical agents. The Gulf War brought out the shortcomings of all present masks and protective clothing. Had Iraq used chemical weapons, the casualties would have been very high.

Dissemination–Vesicants can be distributed by artillery shell, mortar shell, missiles, aircraft spray, and bomb.

Blood Agents–Blood agents are systemic poisons that affect bodily functions by preventing the normal transfer of oxygen from the blood to body tissues. The central nervous system, particularly the respiratory center, is usually susceptible to this interference. Respiratory failure is the usual cause of death. The most important blood agents are hydrocyanic acid (AC) and cyanogen chloride (CK). Inhalation is the usual route of entry.

Hydrocyanic acid is a colorless, highly volatile liquid that has a density 30 percent less than water and is highly soluble and stable in water. AC boils at 26°C (70°F) and freezes at -14°C (7°F). It has a faint odor, like peach kernels or bitter almonds, and sometimes cannot be detected even in lethal concentrations. The action of AC is very rapid, and death occurs within fifteen minutes after a lethal dosage has been received. The rate of detoxification is also very rapid. AC is less persistent than other blood agents and in the gaseous state, is lighter than air. Therefore, the duration of its effectiveness is short.

Cyanogen chloride (CK) in the liquid state is colorless and highly volatile and has a density 18 percent greater than water. Liquid CK boils at 13°C (59°F) and freezes at -7° to -5°C (23° to 20°F). Although it is only slightly soluble in water, it dissolves readily in organic solvents. Its vapor, which is colorless and heavier than air, is very irritating to the eyes and mucous membranes. The pungent, biting odor of CK is masked by its irritating and lacrimatory (tear-producing) properties.

Even though CK is commonly considered a rapid-acting chemical agent, its actual rate of action is not available. It is assumed that the effect of CK arises from its conversion to AC in the body. Its rate of detoxification is rapid. CK will break or penetrate a protective mask canister or filter elements more readily than most other agents, and for this reason, CK has been nicknamed "canister kracker." This action, however, requires very high concentrations of the agent. Normally CK is nonpersistent, and its duration of effectiveness is short. However, its vapor may persist in jungle and forest areas for some time under suitable conditions.

The protective mask gives adequate protection against field concentrations of blood agents, but impermeable clothing, as well as the mask is needed when liquid AC is handled. No decontaminants are required by personnel exposed to AC or CK under field conditions.

AC can be dispersed by mortar shell, bombs, and missiles. CK can be dispersed by mortar shell, bombs, missiles, and grenades.

Choking agents—Certain lung irritants are referred to as choking agents because irritation of the bronchi, trachea, larynx, and nose may occur. This with a pulmonary edema contributes to a choking sensation. In extreme cases, membranes swell, lungs become filled with fluid, and death results from lack of oxygen. In this way, these agents "choke" the victim, and fatalities are referred to as "dry-land drowning." Phosgene (CG) and diphosgene (DP) are lung irritants that typify choking agents. Because DP is converted to CG in the body, the physiological action is the same for both agents.

Phosgene—At normal temperature and pressure, phosgene (CG) is a colorless gas that has an odor resembling that of new-mown hay, freshly cut grass, or green corn. It is readily condensed by pressure or low temperature to a colorless liquid, which boils at 8°C (46°F). Phosgene reacts rapidly with water to produce nontoxic hydrolysis products. Its concentration in air is reduced by water condensates (rain, fog) and by dense vegetation. It has been known as a nonpersistent chemical agent. CG vapor may persist for some time in low places under calm or during light winds and stable atmospheric conditions (inversion).

Although immediate symptoms may follow exposure to high concentrations of CG, three hours or more may elapse before exposure to a low concentration causes any ill effects. CG is not detoxified, and its effects are cumulative. The protective mask provides adequate protection against phosgene. In the field, decontamination is not required. In confined areas, aeration may be of value. Phosgene can be dispersed by mortar shell, bombs, missiles, and cylinders.

Diphosgene–DP has the advantage of a high boiling point, which allows filling shells in the field. CG, having a low boiling point, must be kept refrigerated during the filling operations under summer conditions. DP does have certain disadvantages. Because it is slightly lacrimatory, personnel are not as easily surprised as with CG. The lower volatility of DP adds to the difficulty of setting up an effective surprise concentration. DP can be dispersed by mortar shell, large-caliber artillery shell, bombs, and missiles.

Vomiting agents–Vomiting agents are used for mob and riot control. The three principal agents in this group are diphenylchloroarsine (DA), diphenylaminochloroarsine (Adamsite, DM), and diphenylcyanoarsine (DC). These agents are normally solids which when heated vaporize and then condense to form toxic aerosols. They also produce effects on personnel by inhalation or by direct action on the eyes. Under field conditions, vomiting agents cause great discomfort to their victims. When released indoors, they may cause serious illness and death.

At 20°C, DA is a white to brown solid, DM is a yellow to green solid, and DC is a white to pink solid. When concentrated, DM smoke is canary yellow, DA and DC smokes are white. All three smokes are colorless when diluted with air. Furthermore, low concentration is effective and may not be detectable at the time of exposure. All three agents act very rapidly. DA acts on personnel within two to three minutes after one minute of exposure. DM causes temporary incapacitation after only about one minute of exposure, to a concentration of 22 mg/m^3. High concentrations of DC are intolerable after about thirty seconds.

The rate of detoxification for all three agents is rapid. Any incapacitating amount of DA is detoxified completely within one to two hours. DM is detoxified quite rapidly in small amounts. Incapacitating amounts lose their effect after about thirty minutes. Incapacitating amounts of DC lose their effect after about one hour.

The protective mask gives adequate protection against field concentrations of vomiting agents. No other protective clothing is required, and no decontamination is required in the field. These agents may be dispersed by candles and grenades. Because the agents are dispersed as aerosols, their duration of effectiveness is short.

Tear agents–Tear agents, or lacrimators, are used primarily in training and riot control. Considering the small likelihood of tear agents producing casualties and the effectiveness of the protective mask, these agents have little more than nuisance value in war. Tear agents are local irritants that in very low concentrations act primarily on the eyes, causing intense pain and flow of tears. High concentrations produce irritation of the upper respiratory tract and skin. Examples of tear agents are chloroacetophenone (CN) and O-chlorobenzalmalonitrile (CS).

During the Waco standoff, CS agents were used, and these caused the subsequent fire and death of some eighty people.

CN agent–At normal temperature, CN is a white crystalline solid that is stable in storage and melts at $54^{\circ}C$ ($129^{\circ}F$). It is used sometimes in liquid form by dissolving it in appropriate solvents. This agent may appear as a bluish-white cloud at the point of release. Its odor, if any, may be faint and may resemble apple blossoms.

The vapor pressure of CN is generally so low that although effective lacrimating concentrations can be produced in the field, skin-irritating concentrations do not commonly occur except in enclosed spaces. The rate of action on personnel is practically instantaneous. Detoxification is rapid since effects of CN disappear in a few hours. Because CN is dispersed as an aerosol, the duration of its effectiveness is short. In the field, adequate decontamination is accomplished by aeration. Tear gas in powder form may be used as a persistent harassing agent to deny areas to trespassers.

CS agent–At normal temperature, CS is a white crystalline solid that is stable under ordinary storage conditions and melts at 93° to $95^{\circ}C$. It has a minimum purity of 96 percent and is insoluble in water or ethyl alcohol. It has a pungent, pepperlike odor. The CS cloud is white at the point of release and for several seconds after release. CS is faster acting, more potent, and less toxic than CN.

In terms of weight, the effectiveness of CS is about ten times that of CN. Thus one-tenth of an ounce of CS will produce about the same results as one ounce of CN. The rate of action of CS on personnel is instantaneous. Detoxification is quite rapid because incapacitating dosages lose their effect in five to ten minutes. Area decontamination is not required because CS has a short duration of effectiveness. Personnel exposed to CS may shower as necessary. When CS dust or particles are on the skin, showering should be delayed for six hours to prevent stinging and reddening of the skin.

Protection against CN and CS is provided by the protective mask. For CS, ordinary field clothing secured at the neck, wrist, and ankles can be worn. Personnel handling CS should wear rubber gloves for additional protection.

Solid tear agents are dispersed as a mixture of vapor and fine particulate smoke by burning-type munitions, such as lacrimator candles and grenades. Liquid tear agents may be dispersed from airplane spray or bursting munitions.

Incapacitating agents–Incapacitating agents are capable of producing physiological and mental effects that prevent exposed personnel from performing their primary, military duties for a significant period of time. The two general types of incapacitation that are likely to be encountered in military use are CNS (central nervous system) depressants and CNS stimulants.

BZ agent–BZ is an example of a CNS depressant. This agent is a white crystalline powder that seems to block the action of acetylcholine (a neurotransmitter important for muscle stimulation), both peripherally and centrally. The pharmacological actions of BZ are similar to those of other anticholinergic drugs, such as atropine and scopolamine, but are of longer duration. The action of BZ on the central nervous system disturbs the higher integrative functions of memory, problem solving, attention, and comprehension. High doses produce toxic delirium, which destroys the ability to perform any military task. When BZ enters the body by inhalation, its effects will become evident thirty to sixty minutes after exposure. Its maximum effect will be reached in four to eight hours. Untreated casualties will require two to four days to recover from BZ intoxication.

LSD agent–LSD, or lysergic acid diethylamide, is a CNS stimulant. It is a crystalline solid that induces psychotic symptoms similar to those of schizophrenia. Indoles such as LSD cannot be used to produce delirium in militarily feasible doses. The disturbance produced by LSD is not really delirium because the victim remains receptive to his environment and can comprehend quite well, even though he may have great difficulty reacting appropriately.

It is probable that incapacitating agents will be dispersed by smoke-producing munitions or aerosols, using the respiratory track as an entranceway. The use of the protective mask, therefore, is essential. With some incapacitating agents, the percutaneous (through-the-skin) route may be used, but it is generally less effective.

Emergency Medical Aid
Nerve agent poisoning–Nerve agents are highly effective as quick-acting, casualty producing chemical agents. Characteristics of nerve agents contributing to this effectiveness are ease of entry into the body and the lack of properties that make them immediately and easily detected. Add to this the rapidity with which very small concentrations of nerve agents can produce casualties and death.

Although nerve agents differ in their chemical structure, all of them produce the same physiological effects in man: an imbalance between the sympathetic and parasympathetic nervous systems, which together compose the automatic nervous system. A normal nerve cell metabolism produces a substance called acetylcholine. This substance would continually stimulate the nervous system if it were not normally destroyed by an enzyme called cholinesterase. Nerve agents react with cholinesterase in an irreversible reaction in tissue fluid and inhibit the secretion of the enzyme. Thus cholinesterase is prevented from destroying the accumulation of acetylcholine. The resulting continual stimulation of the nervous system causes the characteristic physiological symptoms.

Very prompt intramuscular injections of atropine can block the action of accumulated acetylcholine on the nervous system, but there is no evidence that this blocking agent reacts chemically with the acetylcholine. Furthermore atropine does not restore the normal action of cholinesterase. The normal functioning of cholinesterase may be restored by administering oximes usually in the form of 2-PAM chloride (protopam chloride or pralidoxime chloride). When this oxime is injected, it reacts with the nerve agent and converts it into a harmless compound. 2-PAM chloride reacts directly with the cholinesterase. This not only protects the enzyme from inhibition, but it also reactivates the inhibited enzyme both in blood and tissue.

Death from nerve-agent poisoning is caused by anoxia (oxygen deficiency) due to respiratory failure, resulting from weakness of the respiration muscles, depression of the central nervous system, and airway obstruction by bronchial and salivary secretions. Atropine dries up secretions in the respiratory tract and stimulates central respiratory functions. 2-PAM chloride should be used simultaneously to relieve muscle paralysis, especially muscles of respiration.

Signs and symptoms–Signs and symptoms characteristic of nerve-agent poisoning are the following:

1. a feeling of tightness or constriction in the chest;

2. the onset of an unexplained runny nose;

3. small, pinpoint-size pupils when exposure is cutaneous (of the skin) or has followed ingestion;

4. a slightly painful sensation in the eyes or unexplained dimness of vision;

5. difficulty breathing;

6. increased salivation and excessive sweating;

7. nausea, vomiting, abdominal cramps, and involuntary defecation and urination;

8. generalized muscular twitching, jerking, and staggering;

9. headache, confusion, drowsiness, convulsions, and coma;

10. cessation of breathing and death.

Generally these signs and symptoms appear in the sequence in which they are listed. However, some degree of variability must be allowed because of such factors as individual difference, the particular nerve agent, concentration of the nerve agent, duration of exposure, and portal of entry.

Probably, inhalation will be the commonest route of exposure to nerve agents, and the most-likely initial symptoms will be a feeling of tightness or constriction in the chest. If nerve agents enter the body by absorption through the skin and the eyes, the initial systemic symptoms may be generalized sweating and muscular twitching, followed by nausea and abdominal cramps. If the mode of entry is ingestion, the first symptoms are likely to be gastrointestinal.

At first indication that a nerve agent is in the air, the exposed individual must immediately don a protective mask and hood, if available. He should stop breathing until the mask is on and the face piece is cleared and checked. The mask should be worn constantly until tests indicate the nerve gas is gone, and the "all clear" signal is given.

Let us discuss protective or gas masks. The ones available on the commercial market are Israeli, older U.S., and German masks. They cost from fifteen to forty dollars. Extra canisters are a must. It helps if you are clean shaven when wearing a gas mask as this will provide a better seal. Once you have purchased a mask, test the fit. This is relatively easy to do without sacrificing a filter. Place the mask over your face, tighten the straps, and place your hand over the opening of your filter. If you start to experience lack of air, your seal is adequate.

Nerve agents can penetrate through the skin. So in addition to a gas mask, you must have a full bodysuit.

Avoid masks with openings for water tubes. They are a potential source of leaks, and unless you have regular drills, they make the masks more complicated to use.

Nerve agents can penetrate through the skin. So in addition to a gas mask, you must have a full bodysuit. These are available in surplus stores, but they must be tested for leaks. Given that most of us lack proper equipment, a simple method is to seal the suit around the gas mask and using a bicycle pump, inflate it. Immerse the inflated suit in a full bathtub. If you observe air bubbles escaping, you have to do some patching.

In general, a gas mask is most useful to wait out a riot when tear gas or pepper spray is used or to escape from a chemical leak in your neighborhood. Unfortunately, they are usually at home when you need them most.

If a liquid nerve agent gets on the skin or clothing, the individual should decontaminate himself as soon as the situation permits. Even so, he should examine the contaminated areas occasionally for local sweating and muscular twitching. If a liquid nerve agent gets in the eye, the eye should be irrigated immediately with water to avoid serious consequences. The protective mask should be put on when the irrigation is completed. Although the eye has been irrigated, the pupil should be watched for about a minute for possible contraction. If there is no mirror available, someone nearby should check out the eye.

Essential therapeutic measures in the treatment of nerve-agent poisoning are:

1. immediate donning of the protective mask and hood, if available, if there is any indication that a nerve agent is in the air;

2. immediate removal of any liquid contamination;

3. immediate administration of atropine when any local or systemic symptoms of a nerve agent are noted. The therapeutic oxime, 2-PAM chloride, should be administered by medical personnel in addition to atropine;

4. removal of bronchial secretions by trained personnel if these are obstructing the airway;

5. administration of artificial respiration, if necessary, and the administration of oxygen, if necessary and available;

6. administration of anticonvulsant drugs by medical personnel if severe and prolonged convulsions are not controlled by atropine.

Except for the specified therapeutic measures, which should be done only by trained personnel, these essential elements of treatment are recommended as self-aid or as first aid. Personnel exposed to high concentrations of a nerve agent may experience loss of coordination, mental confusion, and collapse so rapidly that they will be unable to administer self-aid. If the situation permits, first-aid measures must then be rendered by nearby personnel who may be fortunate enough to be more capable.

The generalized twitching associated with nerve-agent poisoning is followed by severe, generalized weakness of the muscles, including the muscles of respiration. Consequently, breathing becomes progressively more difficult. At first, the breathing of the victim may be shallow and rapid. Then it usually becomes slow and finally intermittent. At this point, there may be physical collapse and unconsciousness followed quickly by cessation of breathing. The subject may die of anoxia within a few minutes unless artificial respiration is started.

Atropine without artificial respiration may save few, if any, in such cases. Artificial respiration without atropine will save many. Artificial respiration plus atropine is the most effective treatment. Casualties with severe poisoning may require several hours of continuous artificial respiration. Usually, when 2-PAM chloride is administered with atropine, the time required for artificial respiration is reduced.

Atropine should not be administered as a preventive measure before contemplated exposure to a nerve agent because the action of atropine may cause an increase in respiratory absorption of the nerve agent by inhibiting bronchi constriction and bronchial secretion.

At the first indication of nerve-agent poisoning and after the protective mask has been donned, the victim should administer to himself a two-milligram intramuscular injection of atropine by means of an automatic injector. Recommended sites for the injection are the thigh or upper arm. If it is not feasible to expose the site of the injection, the injection may be given through uncontaminated clothing. Dryness of the mouth is an indication that enough atropine has been taken to overcome the dangerous effects of the nerve agent. If this kind of relief is obtained and breathing is free, the individual should carry on with his mission.

If the first two-milligram injection of atropine given as a first aid or self-aid does not produce atropinization (dry skin and mouth), two additional two-milligram injections may be given. The doses should be given at twenty-minute intervals if the casualty has mild symptoms of nerve-agent poisoning; at ten-minute intervals if moderate symptoms are present. If the casualty has severe symptoms, as many as six milligrams of atropine may be injected immediately. If the casualty obviously needs more than six milligrams, additional injections may have to be given.

The effects of a two-milligram dose of atropine given intramuscularly begin in about eight minutes and peak in about thirty-five minutes. The effects of atropine are fairly prolonged and last three to five hours after one or two injections and six to twelve hours after four injections at close intervals. Individual differences may influence the degree of side effects produced by atropine. Side effects produced by even one or two injections within one hour may include drowsiness, slowness of memory and ability to recall, the feeling that body movements are slow, and blurring of near vision.

There is usually a complete recovery from nerve-agent poisoning unless anoxia or convulsions have gone unchecked too long and irreversible central nervous system changes occur. However, recovery is not complete until the cholinesterase level has returned to normal. Without 2-PAM chloride, this will require days or weeks. During the period when the cholinesterase level is low, susceptibility to nerve agents is increased, and the effects of repeated exposure are cumulative.

2-PAM chloride has been used successfully alone, or with atropine, for the treatment of nerve-agent poisoning. When practicable, this oxime should be given to every nerve-agent victim as an adjunct to atropine therapy. The administration of 2-PAM chloride does not diminish the importance of artificial respiration in certain cases.

> *Blister agents have a more serious effect than is immediately apparent because signs of injury may not appear for several hours.*

Blister agent effects—While some blister agents (vesicants) have a faint odor, others are odorless. Most blister agents are insidious in action and cause little or no pain at the time of exposure, except lewisite and phosgene oxime, which cause immediate pain on contact. Thus blister agents have a more serious effect than is immediately apparent because signs of injury may not appear for several hours. Furthermore, even very small repeated exposures to mustard are cumulative in effect. For example, repeated exposures to mustard vapors of comparatively low concentration can kill or produce a 100-percent disability. This is done by irritating the lungs and causing a chronic cough and pain in the chest.

Blister agents act on the eyes, lungs, and skin. They burn and blister wherever they touch. They damage the respiratory tract when inhaled and cause vomiting and diarrhea when absorbed. Nitrogen mustards and arsenicals are normally the cause. Moreover, blister agents poison food and water and make other supplies dangerous to handle.

It is significant that Lewinstein mustard (H) and distilled mustard (HD) has casualty effects at lower atmospheric concentrations when the body is moist with perspiration. This is true because wet skin absorbs more mustard than dry skin. Symptoms produced by the action of H, HD, and HN (nitrogen mustard) include:

1. Eyes: conjunctival redness, edema, irritation and gritty pain, inflammation of lids and cornea, lacrimation; blindness, usually temporary and rarely permanent, depending upon the concentration of an agent; myosis (prolonged or excessive contraction of the pupils if other eye symptoms are severe);

2. Skin: redness or rash, intense itching, blisters, ulcer granulation, and sloughing of tissue;

3. Nose and throat: swelling, irritation, ulceration, discharge, an edema (abnormal accumulation of fluid) of the larynx;

4. Respiratory tract: slowly developing irritation, hoarseness, aphonia (loss of voice due to organic or physical causes), cough, tightness, fever, moist rales (respiratory sounds), bronchopneumonia (responsible for almost all deaths following mustard gas exposures), pain, and nausea;

5. Gastrointestinal tract: pain, nausea, vomiting, and diarrhea;

6. Cardiovascular system: systemic shock and bone-marrow damage;

7. Central nervous system: malaise (a vague feeling of physical discomfort or uneasiness), prostration, and depression after severe symptoms.

Lewisite (L) and other arsenical vesicants produce effects similar to those produced by mustard, but local pain and irritation are more prompt and more severe. They are much-more dangerous as liquids than as vapors. The liquids will cause severe burns of the eyes and skin, while field concentrations of vapors are unlikely to cause significant injuries.

Characteristics of lewisite—In order of severity and the appearance of symptoms, lewisite is a blister agent, a toxic lung irritant, and when absorbed in the tissues, a systemic poison. Liquid lewisite causes an immediate searing sensation in the eyes and permanent loss of sight if not decontaminated within one minute. It produces an immediate and strong stinging sensation of the skin. Although reddening of the skin starts within thirty minutes, blistering does not appear until after about thirteen hours. Skin burns produced by lewisite are much deeper than those caused by distilled mustard. Liquid burns appear as grayish splotches. Lewisite can affect the cardiovascular system by producing shock, hemolytic anemia (involving the destruction of red corpuscles, with liberation of hemoglobin into the surrounding fluid), and pulmonary edema. When inhaled in high concentrations, lewisite may be fatal in as soon as ten minutes.

Personnel should wear a protective mask, hood, and protective clothing whenever liquid or vaporized vesicant agents are known to be present. Permeable protective clothing is intended primarily for protection against blister agents, and it is impregnated with chemicals that will neutralize blister agent vapors, aerosols, and small liquid droplets.

Liquid vesicants in the eyes or on the skin require immediate decontamination procedures. The risk of leaving liquid vesicant in the eye is greater than exposure to vesicant vapors. Even during the short period of decontamination, the eyes must be done immediately, despite the presence of vapor. If the contaminated individual is wearing a mask, he should take a very deep breath, hold it before removing the mask, and try to avoid inhalation of vesicant vapor during the brief period needed to flush or irrigate the eye with water.

To flush an eye with water from a canteen or other container of uncontaminated water, the head should be tilted to the side, the eyelids pulled apart with the fingers, and water poured slowly into the eye so that it will run off the side of the face to avoid spread of the contamination. This irrigation must be carried out despite the presence of vesicant vapors in the atmosphere. The breath should be held as long as possible and the mouth kept closed during this procedure to prevent contamination and absorption through mucous membranes.

Skin-decontaminating pads (Fuller's earth) or M5 vesicant agent protective ointment should be used to decontaminate the face and the portion of the mask that met the contamination on the face. Never use them around the eyes as M5 is extremely irritating to the eye.

BAL ointment (dimercaprol) should be tried on arsenical vesicant contaminations of the skin that are seen before actual vesication has begun. This treatment offers an advantage over M5 protective ointment because it penetrates the skin and neutralizes arsenical vesicants in the deeper layers, while the M5 ointment removes only the liquid arsenicals that have not yet penetrated the skin.

Any protective ointment already on the skin must be removed before application of BAL ointment because it destroys the latter. BAL ointment is spread on the skin in a thin film, rubbed in with the fingers, allowed to remain at least five minutes, and later washed off with water. Occasionally, BAL ointment causes stinging, itching, or urticarial wheal, but this condition lasts only an hour or so and should not cause alarm. Mild dermatitis may occur if BAL ointment is frequently applied on the same skin area. This property precludes its use as a protective ointment.

Use of water for phosgene oxime—Because of the rapid reaction of phosgene oxime (CX) with tissue, decontamination will not be entirely effective once pain starts. Despite this fact, the contaminated area should be flushed as rapidly as possible with copious amounts of water to remove any phosgene oxime that has not yet reacted with tissue.

Blisters produced by vesicants should be treated by applying sterile petrolatum gauze. Frequent changes of dressing are undesirable, and the dressing should be left in place as long as possible (up to two weeks). Small blisters on the face are best left alone, but large blisters may be covered with a sterile petrolatum dressing. Burns of the genitalia may be treated with a sterile petrolatum dressing and suspensory, using a minimum of petrolatum. Medical personnel may administer systemic antibiotics.

Erythema or abnormal redness of the skin produced by vesicants may be accompanied by annoying itching. Considerable relief may be obtained by using compound calamine lotion (about 1 percent each of phenol and menthol). Severe erythema is often accompanied by edema, stiffness, and pain.

Clothing that is contaminated with liquid blister agents should be removed and discarded as soon as possible. If removal of the clothing is not feasible, then the contaminated areas should be cut away quickly and discarded or should be decontaminated as rapidly as possible. Decontamination of small areas of the clothing may be accomplished by using M5 protective ointment or by using chloramide powder.

Blood agent effects–Blood agents are systemic poisons that affect bodily functions by combining with cytochrome-oxidase, an enzyme essential for oxidative processes of the tissues. Thus, blood agents prevent the normal transfer of oxygen from the blood to the body tissues. The central nervous system, particularly the respiratory center, is susceptible to this interference. Respiratory failure is the usual cause of death. The most important blood agents are hydrocyanic acid (AC) and cyanogen chloride (CK). While both agents are rapid acting, they are nonpersistent. Inhalation is the usual route of entry.

The symptoms caused by hydrocyanic acid (AC) depend upon the concentrations of the agent and the duration of exposure. Mild exposure may cause headache, giddiness, and nausea, but recovery is complete. Long exposure to low concentrations may cause prolonged tissue anoxia (inadequate oxidation) and damage to the central nervous system. This may lead to convulsions and coma persisting for several hours or days. During recovery there may be residual damage to the central nervous system manifested by irrationality, altered reflexes, and an unsteady gait. These symptoms may last for weeks or longer.

Moderate exposure may rapidly result in giddiness, nausea, and headaches followed by convulsions and coma. High concentrations cause deeper breathing within a few seconds, violent convulsions after twenty to thirty seconds, followed by cessation of regular respiration within one minute, occasional shallow gasps, and finally cessation of heart action only a few minutes after exposure. The initial stimulation of the respiration may be so strong that the victim cannot voluntarily hold his breath. Diagnosis of AC poisoning is suggested by the faint odor (if detected) of peach kernels or bitter almonds, the rapid onset of symptoms, and pink skin color.

The signs and symptoms caused by cyanogen chloride (CK) are a combination of those produced by AC and a lung irritant. The systemic action of CK first stimulates the respiratory center and then rapidly paralyzes it. In high concentrations, its local irritant action may be so great that dyspnea (difficult or labored respiration) is produced. Thus, CK differs from AC in that it causes a slow breathing rate. Exposure is followed by an immediate intense irritation of the nose, throat, and eyes, with coughing, tightness in the chest, and tearing. Afterward, the victim may become dizzy and increasingly dyspneic. Unconsciousness is followed by failing respiration and death within a few minutes.

Convulsions, retching (straining, involuntary effort to vomit), involuntary urination, and defecation may occur. If these effects are not fatal, the signs and symptoms of a pulmonary edema may develop. There may be a persistent cough with much frothy sputum, rales in the chest, severe dyspnea, and marked cyanosis (bluish coloration of the skin caused by lack of oxygen in the blood). Diagnosis of CK poisoning is suggested by the intense irritation and the rapid onset of symptoms.

If there is a sudden stimulation of breathing or an odor like peach kernels or bitter almonds, personnel should suspect the presence of AC and don the protective mask immediately. If personnel become aware of an irritation of the eyes, nose, or throat, they should suspect the presence of CK and don immediately the protective mask. If a person is, in fact, subjected to AC and CK, the treatment should be as follows:

1. Use of amyl nitrite: The first emergency therapeutic measure for blood-agent victims is the inhalation of amyl nitrite.
    If AC or CK is no longer in the surrounding air, two ampules of amyl nitrite should be crushed in the hollow of

the hand and held close to the victim's nose. This may be repeated every few minutes until a total of eight ampules have been used. Artificial respiration should be given if respirations has ceased or is feeble. This will also help the inhalation of amyl nitrite. The artificial respiration must be continued until spontaneous breathing returns or until ten minutes after the last sign of heart activity.

If he is already masked, the crushed ampules of amyl nitrite, in the dosages given above, must then be inserted in the region of the eye lenses of the protective mask, near the deflector-tube openings. The glass ampules are enclosed in cloth coverings that can prevent injury to the eyes from the crushed glass. After the insertion of amyl nitrite, it is important to ensure that the seal of the mask around the face is unbroken. Artificial respiration must be given if the victim is not breathing or if his respiration is feeble.

2. Use of sodium nitrite and sodium thiosulfate: As a second step of emergency treatment, sodium nitrite and sodium thiosulfate should be administered intravenously by medical personnel. Ten milliliters of a 3-percent solution of sodium nitrite should be injected intravenously over a period of one minute. Fifty milliliters of a 25-percent solution of sodium thiosulfate should be given slowly in intravenous injection.

3. Use of oxygen: If oxygen is available, it is suggested for those blood-agent victims who exhibit cyanosis. High concentrations of oxygen should be used initially.

4. Use of water: If a liquid blood agent gets on the skin, it should be blotted off immediately. The contaminated spot should then be washed promptly with soapy water or else flushed with water. If a liquid blood agent enters the eye, the eye should be flushed with water.

If first-aid measures are inadequate, the victim should be kept quiet and comfortably warm until given medical attention. The prognosis for victims of AC is that usually death occurs rapidly or recovery is prompt. Occasionally, where tissue anoxia has been prolonged, residual injury of the central nervous system may persist for weeks, and some damage may be permanent. The prognosis for victims of CK and the recovery from the systemic effects is usually as rapid as in AC poisoning, but there may be a higher incidence of residual damage to the central nervous system. Depending upon the concentration of CK to which the victim has been exposed, the pulmonary effects may develop immediately or may be delayed until the systemic effects have subsided.

Choking agent effects—Any chemical agents that attack lung tissue, primarily causing a pulmonary edema, are classed as lung irritants. On this basis, lung irritants include phosgene, cyanogen chloride, chloropicrin, and chlorine. Furthermore, vesicants and certain systemic agents may also injure the respiratory tract. Certain lung irritants are called choking agents because irritation of the bronchi, trachea, larynx, pharynx, and nose may occur and with a pulmonary edema, contribute to a sensation of choking. Phosgene (CG) and diphosgene (DP) are lung irritants that typify choking agents.

When a lethal amount of CG is received, the air sacs become so flooded that air is excluded and the victim dies of anoxia.

CG is primarily harmful to the lungs and is damaging to the capillaries. It causes seepage of watery fluid into the air sacs. When a lethal amount of CG is received, the air sacs become so flooded that air is excluded and the victim dies of anoxia (oxygen deficiency). However, if the amount of CG received is less than lethal and proper care is provided, the watery fluid is reabsorbed, the air cell walls heal, and the patient recovers.

During and immediately after exposure to CG, symptoms are likely to include dryness of throat, coughing, choking, a feeling of tightness in the chest, nausea and occasionally vomiting, headaches, and lacrimation. The presence or absence of these early symptoms does not necessarily show the ultimate effect on the victim. For example, some victims with severe cough fail to develop serious lung injury, while others with no signs of early respiratory tract irritation go on to a fatal pulmonary edema.

There may be an initial slowing of the pulse followed by an increase in the rate. A period follows during which abnormal chest signs are absent and the patient may be free of symptoms. This interval commonly lasts two to twenty-four hours, but is occasionally shorter. It is ended by the signs and symptoms of a pulmonary edema. Most deaths occur within forty-eight hours after exposure. Casualties from phosgene who survive more than 48 hours usually recover without any aftereffects.

Upon suspecting the presence of CG or DP in the air, the person should don the protective mask immediately. Suspicion should be aroused by irritation of the eyes, change in the taste of a cigarette (smoking may become tasteless or offensive in taste), or the odor of freshly cut hay, newly mown grass, or green corn.

Vomiting agent effects–Vomiting agents are used for mob and riot control. Under field conditions, vomiting agents cause great discomfort to their victims. When released indoors they may cause serious illness and death.

Effects produced by DA, DM, and DC stated in progressive order are: irritation of the eyes and mucous membranes, viscous discharge from the nose similar to that caused by a cold, sneezing and coughing, severe headaches, acute pain and tightness in the chest, nausea and vomiting. Mental depression may occur during the progression of symptoms. For moderate concentrations, the effects last about thirty minutes after the victim leaves the contaminated area. At higher concentrations, the effects may last up to several hours.

The onset of symptoms may be delayed for several minutes after initial exposure, especially with DM. Effective exposure may, therefore, have occurred before the presence of the agent is suspected. If the mask is then put on, symptoms will increase for several minutes in spite of adequate protection. Consequently, the victim may believe his mask is ineffective, and by removing it, he may be further exposed.

Upon suspecting the presence of a vomiting agent in the air, personnel should don the protective mask immediately. Suspicion should be aroused by the concurrence of respiratory and eye irritation with nausea. The mask should be worn in spite of coughing, sneezing, salivation, and nausea. The mask should be lifted from the face briefly if it is necessary to allow vomiting or to drain saliva from the face piece.

Since recovery is usually prompt, few cases should require medical attention. Aspirin may be given to relieve headache and general discomfort. Frequent but carefully controlled inhalations of chloroform give symptomatic relief. The victim can inhale the vapor directly from a bottle of chloroform or pour a few drops into the cupped palm of the hand and then inhale the vapor. However, he should understand that since chloroform itself is toxic, it is to be used only to control the symptoms and *not* to the point of inducing anesthesia.

Tear agent effects–Tear agents or lacrimators are local irritants that in very low concentrations act primarily on the eyes causing intense pain and flow of tears. High concentrations produce irritation of the upper respiratory tract and skin. CS may be used in combat.

The effects of CS are felt almost immediately and incapacitation begins in 20-60 seconds. The effects last five to ten minutes after the individual is exposed to fresh air. During this time, the victim is incapable of effective concerted action. Symptoms include burning of the eyes, copious flow of tears, involuntary closing of the eyes, sinus and nasal drip, coughing, difficult breathing, and tightness of the chest. Following exposure to high concentrations of CS, there is nausea and vomiting.

Besides causing powerful lacrimation, CN acts as an irritant to the upper respiratory passages. Higher concentrations are irritating to the skin and cause a burning and itching sensation, especially on the moist parts of the body. Generalized dermatitis may occur rarely with sweating skin. High concentrations can cause blisters. The effects of CN usually disappear in a few hours. After exposure to CN, some individuals may experience nausea. Liquid or solid lacrimators in the eyes are corrosive and produce burns resembling those of strong acids.

Tear-agent victims should don a protective mask and keep the eyes open as much as possible. When vision clears, they should carry on. When it is safe to do so, they should remove the mask and blot away tears without rubbing. The pain and conjunctival irritation caused by lacrimator vapor ordinarily do not require treatment. Nevertheless, burning of the eyes and skin after exposure to lacrimator vapor may be relieved when feasible by washing the eyes with water and washing the skin with soap and water. If a liquid or solid lacrimator enters the eyes (a rare occurrence), the eye should be held open forcibly and flushed out with water. Dermatitis and superficial skin burns may be treated with compound calamine lotion for symptomatic relief.

Incapacitating agent effects–These agents can produce physiological and mental effects that prevent personnel from doing their duties. Both BZ and LSD cause restlessness, giddiness, failure to obey orders, confusion, erratic behavior, stumbling or staggering, and vomiting. In addition, BZ produces dryness of the mouth, tachycardia (abnormally fast heartbeat) at rest, elevated temperature, flushing of face, blurred vision, pupillary dilation, slurred or nonsensical speech, hallucinatory behavior, disrobing, mumbling and picking behavior, stupor, and coma.

LSD produces inappropriate smiling or laughing, irrational fear, destructibility, difficulty expressing oneself, perceptual distortions, unstable increase in pupil size, heart rate, and blood pressure, stomach cramps, and vomiting.

After exposure to incapacitating agents, personnel should decontaminate themselves with soap and water at the earliest opportunity. Even if the skin is washed within an hour, symptoms may appear as late as thirty-six hours after exposure. In fact, a delay in the onset of several hours is typical.

The following are important considerations when rendering first aid to victims of incapacitating agents:

1. If the victim is in a stupor or coma, be sure that his respiration is unobstructed. Moreover, turn him on his side with head to the side to avoid aspiration in case vomiting should occur.

2. If body temperature is elevated above 102°F and mucous membranes are dry, immediate and vigorous cooling, as for a heat stroke, must begin. Such cases are almost always the result of anticholinergic (for example, BZ) intoxication.

3. If the victim appears to comprehend what is being said to him, reassurance and a firm, but friendly attitude will be beneficial. However, if the victim is incoherent or cannot comprehend what is being said, conversation is obviously a waste of time.

4. Although alarming, dryness and coating of the lips and tongue may result from anticholinergic poisoning. There is usually no danger of immediate dehydration. Therefore, if fluids are given at all, they should be given sparingly because of the danger of vomiting and the likelihood of temporary, urinary retention, due to the paralysis of the bladder and smooth muscle. Cleansing the mouth with an astringent swab may be comforting and will reduce the foul breath associated with parching of the membranes.

5. Weapons and other potentially harmful materials should be removed from the possession of individuals who are suspected casualties. These materials should include cigarettes, matches, medications, and various small items that might be

ingested accidentally. Delirious victims have been known to attempt to eat items bearing only superficial resemblance to food.

Chemical agent detection kits–If you are fortunate enough to have these, follow the directions given on the detector kits. There are so many from different countries issued over such a large time frame that any discussion can be only general.

Decontamination

Decontaminating agent, STB (supertropical bleach)–It is a mixture of chlorinated lime and calcium oxide in a white powder form. When freshly manufactured, STB contains 30 percent chlorine. This decontaminant decomposes slowly in storage, giving off a chlorinelike odor.

STB decontaminates G and V nerve agents, mustard and lewisite. STB reacts violently with liquid mustard, and the reaction usually produces enough heat to cause a flame. Mixing STB with water or dirt eases its distribution and reduces heat from the mustard reaction.

To use in a slurry form, mix equal parts by weight with water. STB is corrosive to most metals and should be rinsed immediately and thoroughly from metal surfaces. Metal surfaces should then be oiled. Several applications of the STB may be required when decontaminating porous surfaces such as wood.

Decontaminating agent DS2–This is a clear amber liquid with an odor somewhat resembling ammonia. It neutralizes GB and HD in five minutes. It will soften paint and leather and will damage woolen fabric. It is irritating to the eyes, and a protective mask should be worn during application.

Other decontaminants: Caustic Soda, five-percent solution; soap and detergents; washing soda; organic solvents.

CHEMICAL ATTACKS

Chemical agent decontamination methods

CONTAMINATED SURFACE	RECOMMENDED METHODS OF DECONTAMINATION
Asphalt roads	Flush with water or spray with slurry from power-driven decontaminating apparatus, **or** cover small areas or paths with 10-cm (4") of earth. Weather. **Or** cover with STB. When a liquid contaminant is visible and personnel are nearby, use dry mix.
Asphalt roofs	Flush with water **or** spray with slurry from power-driven decontaminating apparatus. Weather. **Or** cover with STB or dry mix.
Brick and stone roads	Spray with slurry from power-driven decontaminating apparatus, **or** apply with brushes and brooms. Let remain 24 hours, then flush with water. Weather. **Or** wash with soapy water, preferably hot. Cover small areas or paths with 10 cm (4") of earth.
Brick and stone buildings	Spray with slurry from power-driven decontaminating apparatus **or** apply with brushes and brooms. Let remain 24 hours, then flush with water. **Or** use STB or dry mix around buildings where wastewater runs, **or** wash with soapy water, preferably hot. Weather.
Canvas: tarpaulins, tents, covers, mask carriers, cartridge belts	Immerse in boiling soapy water for 1 hour **or** use 5% solution of washing soda for G-agents **or** use slurry. **Or** aerate (except for V-agents), **or** launder by standard methods, **or** use chloramide powder from M13 kit or M5 protective ointment.
Concrete, roads and buildings	Spray with slurry from power-driven decontaminating apparatus. Weather. **Or** cover with STB or dry mix. Cover small areas or paths with 10 cm (4") of earth.
Earth: roads, bivouac areas, pathways, bomb craters	Spray with slurry from power-driven decontaminating apparatus. Cover small areas with 10 cm of earth. Scrape layers of contaminated earth to side of the road. **Or** cover with STB. When a liquid contaminant is visible and personnel are nearby, use dry mix. Weather **or** burn.

Glass lenses	Use DS2, **or** wash with hot soapy water, **or** aerate. **Or** wash with clear water or organic solvent. Blot off surfaces.
Windows	Use DS2, **or** wash with clean water or organic solvent, **or** wash with hot soapy water. Aerate. Weather.
Grass and low vegetation (fields or open terrain)	Burn, **or** spray with slurry from power-driven decontaminating apparatus, **or** explode drums of STB. Cover with STB **or** dry mix. Clear paths through area by use of detonating cord or other detonating devices.
Metals (painted): vehicles, weapons, and equipment	Use DS2. Weather. Aerate. **Or** wash with hot soapy water and rinse. (Slurry may be used if it is removed from surfaces after 1 hour and surface is oiled.)
Unpainted metals, ammunition	Use DS2, then rinse, **or** wipe with organic solvent and dry, **or** wash with cool soapy water and rinse. Aerate.
Machinery	Use DS2 and rinse, **or** wash with organic solvent, **or** wash with hot soapy water. Weather. Aerate.
Mess gear, canned rations	Immerse in boiling soapy water for 30 minutes and rinse **or** spray with DS2 and rinse. **Or** wash in hot soapy water and aerate.
Plastics (opaque): insulation, panels, telephones	Wash with hot soapy water and rinse. Weather. Aerate.
Plastics (transparent)	Spray with DS2 and rinse, **or** aerate. **Or** wash with warm soapy water.
Sand (beaches, desert)	Flush with water, **or** spread STB or spray over the surface. Weather. Cover paths with roofing paper. **Or** scrape off 10 cm (4") of contaminated top layer.
Undergrowth and tall grass (meadows, jungles, forests)	Spray slurry from power-driven decontaminating apparatus, **or** burn. Weather. **Or** explode drums of STB. Clear paths with detonating cord, bangalore torpedoes, or demolition snakes.

CHEMICAL ATTACKS

Wood buildings	Apply slurry with power-driven decontaminating apparatus, brooms, or swabs. Let slurry remain 12-24 hours, flush and repeat, then flush again. **Or** scrub with hot and soapy water and rinse. Weather.
Boxes, crates, gunstocks	Apply slurry as above. Weather. **Or** use chloramide powder from M13 kit for gunstocks.
Painted wood surfaces	Apply slurry as above, **or** use DS2 and rinse, **or** scrub with hot water and rinse. Weather.

8
NUCLEAR SURVIVAL

Since September 11, 2001, we must consider another possible terrorist method of attack. This involves the use of spent nuclear fuel canisters. Nuclear power generating stations are well protected, lately even having ground-to-air missile batteries to knock down any plane attempting to crash into the facility.

In contrast, the protection of spent nuclear fuel storage depots leaves a lot to be desired. At its simplest, a stolen canister is embedded in a concrete traffic barrier, delivered to make Washington "safer." Later an explosive charge spews the contents around a major city, exposing thousands of people to high radiation damage. And unless all the material is recovered, the area will be denied to people for a long time.

Given the planning ability shown in the case of the planes turned into bombs, it's entirely feasible that such a plan has already been considered. To reduce the probability of such an event, we must guard the spent nuclear fuel sites much more vigorously.

With the arrival of nuclear weapons, for the first time humanity can destroy the planet's ecosystem. As long as nation-states possess these weapons in large quantities, the danger of nuclear war exists. Many say that with the arrival of nuclear weapons, war is obsolete. The nitrous oxides thrown up in the stratosphere can actually diminish the life-protecting ozone layer by 70 percent or more in the Northern Hemisphere and up to 50 percent in the Southern Hemisphere. This would result in extinction for much of the animal kingdom, plants, and even creatures of the sea. In preparing this book, we realized the awful destruction possible from an all-out nuclear war. We pray that it won't happen.

With the changes in the political scene, in particular the break up of the USSR, this chapter is predicated upon a limited nuclear war or a terrorist group exploding a nuclear power generation plant. When the Cold War ended, many of us felt like tearing up our survival plans. Alas, now we have more dangerous owners of a limited number of very dirty nuclear weapons. Limited nuclear war survival in most respects is very similar to survival situations discussed before. However, there are several major differences. If you ignore these, then your chances of being a survivor will be severely diminished.

Foremost is the lack of warning time. Should intercontinental ballistic missiles be used, your warning time is at most thirty minutes. The suddenness of a nuclear exchange may find you away from your family, home, and supplies. Your plan must consider this. Many suggest moving to your retreat or your shelter when the international situation becomes very tense. This is difficult for most of us given work commitments and the like.

Another aspect of nuclear war lies in the amount of radioactivity it produces. This is something you cannot see, taste, smell, touch, or hear. Therefore having radiation detection instruments is essential on your list of equipment. Having a personal dosimeter to show the amount of radiation your body has accumulated is also desirable. If you don't have one, you must keep track of the radiation readings you make and calculate how much radiation you have been exposed to.

The speed at which destruction is caused by a nuclear exchange between nations negates many plans for moving to your retreat until after the radioactivity decays sufficiently to allow limited travel. Should you be able to foretell the timing of such an attack, then you are very fortunate, indeed.

There are certain signs that may suggest to you that nuclear war may come. Between the two superpowers, there was an established escalation ladder. As a general guide, we are including the one prepared by Herman Kahn.

Disagreement-Cold War
Subcrisis maneuvering
1. Ostensible crisis
2. Political, economic, and diplomatic gestures
3. Solemn and formal declarations

Don't rock the boat threshold
Traditional crises
4. Hardening of positions, confrontation of wills
5. Show of force
6. Significant mobilization
7. "Legal" harassment–retaliations
8. Harassing acts of violence
9. Dramatic military confrontations

Nuclear war is unthinkable threshold
Intense crises
10. Provocative breaking off of diplomatic relations
11. Super-ready status
12. Large conventional war (or actions)
13. Large compound escalation
14. Declaration of limited conventional war
15. Barely nuclear war
16. Nuclear "ultimatums"
17. Limited evacuation (approximately 20 percent)
18. Spectacular show or demonstration of force
19. "Justifiable" counterforce attack
20. "Peaceful" worldwide embargo or blockade

No nuclear use threshold
Bizarre crises
21. Local nuclear war–exemplary
22. Declaration of limited nuclear war
23. Local nuclear war–military
24. Unusual, provocative, and significant countermeasures
25. Evacuation (approximately 70 percent)

Central sanctuary threshold
Exemplary central attack
26. Demonstration attack on zone of interior
27. Exemplary attack on the military
28. Exemplary attacks against property
29. Exemplary attacks on population
30. Complete evacuation (approximately 95 percent)
31. Reciprocal reprisals

Central war threshold
Military central wars
32. Formal declaration of "general" war
33. Slow-motion, counterproperty war
34. Slow-motion, counterforce war
35. Constrained force-reduction salvo
36. Constrained disarming attack
37. Counterforce with avoidance attack
38. Unmodified counterforce attack

City targeting threshold
Civilian central wars
39. Slow-motion, countercity war
40. Countervalue salvo
41. Augmented disarming attack
42. Civilian devastation attack
43. Some other kinds of controlled general war
44. Spasm or insensate war

Aftermath
Having read the list, you may be tempted to say, "All right, I will bug out between steps twenty-five and twenty-six." Alas, life is not so simple. First, the escalation ladder may not be followed step-by-step. Second, the timing of escalation can be slow or very fast. In a conventional war situation, a large loss by one side may result in that side using nuclear weapons. The escalating tensions between India and Pakistan are hard to pigeonhole.

The third complicating factor lies in the spread of nuclear weapons technology and capability to many, sometimes unstable countries. One cannot rule out the use of nuclear devices by terrorist groups. If you perceive such a possibility happening, you must evaluate whether you live in a target area.

NUCLEAR SURVIVAL

What is a target area? Anything and everything the enemy feels will hamper you from attacking and/or defending. A short list of targets in descending order of importance is shown below:

- Strategic nuclear forces, air, sea, land
- Early warning sites and command posts
- Military headquarters and depots
- National capitals
- Major sea- and airports, railroad centers
- Nuclear weapons assembly plants
- Tactical weapons assembly plants
- Major industrial centers
- Major population centers
- Dams, power-distribution centers

Most of us, by necessity, live in an area close to one of the possible targets listed above. Your plan should include figuring out the likelihood of your vicinity becoming a target. This depends on how many nuclear weapons and delivery vehicles the other side has. For example, if a terrorist group has a single device, then Minneapolis is not a likely target. However, if the antagonist is Russia, you may have to think twice about staying there.

In many ways, you must become an armchair general. Keeping a close eye on world events and how they may impact your well-being will have to be second nature to you. Another vital consideration is how your government reacts to external threats. Should your government, in response to external threats, curtail movement of people and/or goods, you may have to move early to retain your freedoms.

Now that we have covered the overview of nuclear war possibilities, let us get down to the details. It should be possible to gain some advance warning of the imminence of future hostilities involving the North American continent (including nuclear war) by maintaining an intelligent surveillance of current events as portrayed by the news media. A deteriorating international situation, prolonged famine, drought, hostile propaganda aimed increasingly at the U.S.A., and accusations of military aggression are so commonplace that we scarcely pay them attention. However, when you start hearing about withdrawal of diplomatic personnel, economic collapse in one of the technologically advanced nations, or the use of chemical or nuclear devices against countries, then these could indicate that war may be more imminent. A major war once started may rapidly deteriorate into a nuclear holocaust.

If in your assessment the situation has become critical, put your personal survival plan into action as soon as you reach a decision. In a major conflict involving the use of nuclear weapons, you can expect only a thirty-minute warning of an impending strike and maybe not even that long. All early warning systems are geared to allow sufficient time to launch an immediate military counterstrike, while the warning broadcast to the civilian population can't be given until the knowledge of an impending strike has percolated down through a variety of government levels.

Once a nuclear attack has been confirmed, a yellow alert (attack probable) may be broadcast on a nationwide basis or even a red alert (attack underway). However, this information must filter through the military system down to the Regional Defense Centers to the community level, if communities still have operational civil defense organizations—most of them don't. Finally, the sirens will sound, and the news will be broadcast. Unfortunately, most sirens have been disconnected or removed, and most people would complain of noise pollution if they heard them being tested.

Unless you are in the know, this is the best you can hope for. However, the military advantage to be gained by surprise is such that in all probability the warheads will be detonating before any warning can be given. In any event, the various civil defense organizations in both the U.S. and Canada have been quietly disintegrating into complete uselessness for many years. So unless upgrading occurs, which is not very likely, you can accept the fact that once the bombs start falling you are pretty much on your own.

When and if the sirens sound, the alert warning in both the U.S.A. and Canada is of a three-minute duration. The take cover siren is either an undulating tone or a series of short tones. In Canada, there is an additional signal, the alert repeat, which is a fallout warning. Chances are that any type of message signaled by the sirens will be ignored by the majority of the populace. This is not idle speculation.

Understanding that war is possible, people may be inclined to accept such warnings as real. One can only hope that at the same time sirens are sounded, there will be radio and TV broadcasts. However, sad experience shows that the likeliest result of the sirens and the various broadcasts will be to immediately shut down most telephone networks. That's because every idiot with a telephone grabs it to call police, radio and television stations, politicians, and civil defense numbers to double-check the news.

From this point on, the domestic situation will deteriorate. Continued warning broadcasts from major centers will cease, either because those centers become targets or their personnel leave the stations to find shelters. Each community throughout the continent then becomes isolated for the duration of the attack, and people are dependent upon their own resources to survive.

Given today's media hype of overstating events, the majority of the population will only accept the attack as factual when the mushroom-shaped clouds start to make their appearance on the horizon. Then panic will strike, and a frenzied rush will be made for shelter—any kind of shelter—while frantic citizens desperately try to recall fragments of half-forgotten civil defense procedures.

The knowledge of nuclear survival does not exist in the public mind anymore.

Remember, an entire generation has grown up and married since civil defense and the imminence of a possible nuclear war were last in vogue. The knowledge of nuclear survival does not exist in the public mind anymore. As a potential survivor, you must face the facts. If you do not get sufficient knowledge to survive now, let alone make some definite physical preparations, survival of a nuclear strike will be simply impossible.

In regard to nuclear explosions, mechanically speaking, a nuclear detonation is not much different from a conventional chemical explosion other than in the production of radioactivity. The scale of the explosion, in comparison to the capabilities of conventional weapons, is staggering. But it is only a magnification of the same series of physical stages. For example, the atomic bomb dropped on Hiroshima during the closing days of World War II was a nominal twenty-kiloton weapon. That means apart from its capability to produce radioactive particles, its explosive weight in terms of conventional chemical explosives was in the region of twenty thousand tons of TNT.

Since 1945, nuclear weapon development has progressed considerably, and with the development of the hydrogen bomb, weapons in the megaton range are now commonly found in the arsenals of the various nuclear powers. Fortunately, the larger devices require more effort to deliver to a target. It is considered that should nuclear war take place the ten-megaton systems are likely to predominate in the heavy class at least.

When we start talking about the equivalent of ten million tons of TNT and perhaps include the possibility of more than one nuclear strike in the same area, the figures tend to become meaningless. The important fact is that in spite of the size of a nuclear weapon detonation of any type, you can survive unless you are at ground zero.

The particular location on the earth's surface at or above which a nuclear device is detonated is called ground zero and is commonly abbreviated with the initials G.Z. It is still G.Z. even when the device is triggered several thousands of feet up in the air. Normally, this would only be a matter of abstract technical interest were it not for the fact that a device triggered several thousand feet above ground level (an air burst) has more destructive impact on soft targets. By the way, a soft target is your home. The air burst, in addition to its greater destructive efficiency over a wider area, is relatively clean inasmuch as it does not produce as much radioactive fallout as a surface burst.

A surface or ground burst is employed on hardened military installations. The nuclear device upon detonation throws up thousands of tons of dirt and debris. The dirt being irradiated becomes radioactive particles, later to be released as fallout. This causes major, long-term problems for the survivors.

This is what happens when a ten-megaton nuclear device is detonated at ground level. The initial explosion makes a crater half a mile in diameter and 250 feet deep. Simultaneously, a fireball three miles in diameter is formed, thirty times more brilliant than the sun. It is capable of permanently blinding a human being looking directly at it sixty miles away, and it will last almost one minute.

Within ten minutes, the familiar mushroom-shaped cloud, fifty miles in diameter and more than twenty miles high, will have formed. The cloud basically consists of thousands upon thousands of tons of dirt and debris pulverized by the initial explosion that is now being sucked up into the cloud and made radioactive.

Concurrent with the initial explosion and formation of the fireball, a tremendous shockwave is produced, which spreads outwards from ground zero at a speed of 770 miles per hour. This falls to 275 miles per hour at a distance of five miles from G.Z. and to 100 miles per hour at eight miles from G.Z. Initially, it will smash the strongest buildings to fragments, its capability being progressively reduced as it loses speed.

Within five miles of ground zero, destruction of all buildings will be complete and fires caused by the intense heat of the fireball will be blazing. Survival within this area is well-nigh improbable. At ten miles from G.Z., destruction of property will be so extensive that repair is impossible. Fires caused by the explosion will be common, and the survival rate will be about 50 percent. Practically speaking, if you were not under cover in this area at the moment of impact, you would survive only by accident.

At a distance of fifteen miles from ground zero, wooden structures such as frame houses would receive extensive, but repairable damage. Most people would survive, even outdoors, although direct exposure to the light of the fireball would produce second-degree burns on exposed areas of flesh.

At a distance of eighteen miles from G.Z., the shock wave would still be capable of causing structural damage and some deaths. Even at sixty miles from G.Z. various forms of light damage such as broken windows may be expected. This is in addition to retinal burns among individuals who may have watched the detonation. Properly protected, you can survive the blast and heat to within five miles of ground zero.

Because heat is applied only for a matter of seconds, light-weight, easily kindled materials are most likely to ignite. Surveys done in the 1960s show that typical American cities contain five to twenty-five points per acre where fires may begin from thermal radiation. The point system was devised based upon the typical construction materials found in American towns. Although it's hard to predict precisely, there is a danger that many small fires could merge into a single, great "firestorm" with strong updrafts at the center creating violent cyclonic winds. This is akin to what happened during World War II in Dresden.

Thermal radiation travels like light. Ducking quickly into shadowed area or covering the exposed skin with clothing offers some personal protection. Sound travels similarly, and close to G.Z., it can burst the eardrums.

Another way of looking at the heat effects from an air burst is shown in the table below.

Heat vs. range of nuclear weapons effects
(Numbers are in miles)

Weapon Yield	Metal Vaporizes	Metal Melts	Plastic Burns	3rd Degree Burns	2nd Degree Burns	1st Degree Burns
10 Kt	0.2	0.5	0.8	1.2	1.7	2.9
20 Kt	0.3	0.6	1.2	1.7	2.2	3.8
50 Kt	0.5	0.9	1.9	2.7	3.6	6
100 Kt	0.7	1.3	2.7	3.6	5	8.5
200 Kt	0.9	1.8	3.6	5	8	11.9
500 Kt	1.4	2.8	5.5	8.5	10.5	18.5
1 Mt	2	3.9	8.3	10.7	15	25
10 Mt	6	11.9	24.5	33	46	80
100 Mt	18	35	75	112	50	255

Pressure changes—The blast wave starts as a high-pressure shock front, traveling somewhat faster than the speed of sound. After a few seconds, a negative-pressure phase follows. The effect is twofold, first compressing and then expanding or exploding structures and human tissue. As the blast wave travels away from its source and the overpressure at the front steadily decreases, the pressure behind also falls off in a similar manner. After a short time when the shock front has traveled a certain distance from the fireball, the pressure behind drops below that of the surrounding atmosphere. At this point, the so-called "negative phase" of the blast wave forms. In the region where the air pressure is below that of the original (or ambient) atmosphere, an "underpressure" is created. This acts like a partial vacuum.

During the negative (rarefaction or suction) phase when the partial vacuum is produced, the air is sucked in. In the positive (or compression) phase, the wind associated with a blast wave blows away from the explosion. At the end of the negative phase, which is somewhat longer than the positive phase, the pressure has essentially returned to ambient. Generally the peak values of the underpressures are small in comparison with the peak overpressures, and they can be expected to have a maximum value of about four pounds per square inch below that of ambient pressure.

Along with these great swings in pressure, there would be short wind gusts of enormous velocity—up to 1,000 mph near ground zero. Drag forces of these winds do much of the damage to buildings and the bulk of blast injuries to humans. At that velocity, even wood splinters will penetrate like bullets.

Note: Near ground zero, pressures and winds are higher in a surface burst than an air burst. Farther out, an air burst creates stronger pressures and winds because the blast wave bounces off the earth and reinforces the primary wave to create the so-called *mach front.*

Dynamic pressure—The destructive effects of blast waves are related not only to values of peak overpressure, but also to another quantity of equivalent importance called the dynamic pressure. Dynamic pressure is the air pressure that results from the mass air flow (or wind) behind the shock front as it impinges on an object or structure. The degree of blast damage to a great variety of buildings depends largely on the drag force associated with the strong transient winds accompanying the passage of the blast wave. Although the drag force is influenced by the shape and size of a structure, it is generally dependent upon the peak value of the dynamic pressure and its duration at a given location.

Damage to types of structures primarily affected by overpressure

Description of Structure	Severe Damage	Moderate Damage
Multistory, reinforced concrete walls, blast-resistant design for 30 psi, 1 MT bomb, no windows	Walls shattered; severe frame distortion; incipient collapse.	Walls breached or on the point of being so; frames distorted. Entranceways damaged; doors blown in or jammed; extensive spalling (chipping or splintering) of concrete.
Multistory, reinforced concrete building with concrete walls, small window area, 3 to 8 stories	Walls shattered; severe frame distortion; incipient collapse.	Exterior walls badly cracked; interior partitions badly cracked or blown down. Structural frames permanently distorted; extensive spalling of concrete.
Multistory, wall-bearing building, brick apartment house type, up to 3 stories	Bearing walls collapse, resulting in total collapse of structure.	Exterior walls facing blast badly cracked; interior partitions badly cracked or blown down.

Multistory, wall-bearing building, monumental type, up to four stories	Bearing walls collapse, resulting in collapse of structure supported by these walls; some bearing walls may be shielded enough by intervening walls so that part of the structure may receive only moderate damage.	Exterior walls facing blast badly cracked; interior partitions badly cracked; less damage toward the far end of the building.
Wood-frame building, house type, 1 or 2 stories	Frames shattered so that structure for the most part collapses.	Wall framing cracked; roofs badly damaged; interior partitions blown down.

Damage to types of structures primarily affected by pressure during the drag phase

DESCRIPTION OF STRUCTURE	SEVERE DAMAGE	MODERATE DAMAGE
Light steel-frame industrial building, single story with up to 5-ton crane capacity	Severe distortion or collapse of the frame.	Some to major distortion of frame; cranes (if any) not operable until repairs are made.
Heavy steel-frame industrial building, single story with 25-50 ton crane capacity	Severe distortion or collapse of the frame.	Some distortion to frame; cranes not operable until repairs are made.
Heavy steel-frame industrial building, single story with 60-100 ton crane capacity	Severe distortion or collapse of the frame.	Some distortion to frame; cranes not operable until repairs are made.

Multistory, steel-frame, office-type building, 3-10 stories (earthquake-resistant construction)	Severe frame distortion, incipient collapse.	Frames distorted moderately; interior partitions are blown down.
Multistory, steel-frame, office-type building, 3-10 stories (non-earthquake-resistant construction)	Severe frame distortion, incipient collapse.	Frames distorted moderately; interior partitions are blown down.
Multistory, reinforced concrete, frame, office-type building, 3-10 stories (earthquake-resistant construction)	Severe frame distortion, incipient collapse.	Frames distorted moderately; interior partitions blown down; some spalling of concrete.
Multistory, reinforced concrete, frame, office-type building, 3-10 stories (non-earthquake-resistant construction)	Severe frame distortion, incipient collapse.	Frames distorted moderately; interior partitions blown down; some spalling of concrete.
Highway truss bridges, spans 150-250 feet	Total failure of lateral bracing; collapse of bridge.	Some failure of lateral bracing such that bridge capacity is reduced about 50%.
Railroad truss bridges, spans 150-250 feet	Total failure of lateral bracing; collapse of bridge.	Some failure of lateral bracing such that bridge capacity is reduced about 50%.
Highway and railroad truss bridges, spans 250-500 feet	Total failure of lateral bracing; collapse of bridge.	Some failure of lateral bracing such that bridge capacity is reduced about 60%.

Neutron bombs–The most-recent development in the nuclear arms field is the much-discussed neutron bomb, which is dependent to a far-greater extent than earlier nuclear weapons upon the release of immediate radiation of extremely high intensity. This is in contrast to the heat and blast effects of the more-conventional nuclear devices. Only the U.S.A. possesses these weapons in any number. At this time, they are not a threat to us.

Aftermaths–In a nuclear confrontation from the viewpoint of immediate personal survival, the second-strike detonations will result in an increase in both the length and intensity of radioactivity. This requires the survivor to spend an extended period in a fallout shelter. The implication, of course, is that you stock your shelter for a minimum of one month's residence rather than the two weeks advocated by civil defense literature. In all seriousness, you had better plan on storing sufficient supplies and equipment to last you for a hell of a lot longer than even a month. We have not said a word about "nuclear winter" yet. Those supplies will also have to feed you and your family for an unknown length of time even after you leave the shelter.

The debris sucked up to form the mushroom cloud in a nuclear explosion is later released with interest. Eventually, it falls back to earth under the influence of gravity. It forms a pattern on the ground dictated by the particle size and prevailing winds. All of it has been rendered strongly radioactive and is known as the fallout.

It will start to drop back to earth within fifteen minutes of detonation, heavier particles first. It will continue to do so for the following three or four days. Since the general direction of high-level air currents over the North American continent is from west to east, the fallout will result in the formation of cigar-shaped patterns. The pattern typically will be 150 miles long, east of G.Z., with one end of the cigar originating at the point of detonation.

For immediate survival purposes, we may consider the three different classes of radiation being emitted by the fallout particles. They are alpha particles, beta particles, and gamma rays. Alpha and beta particles are dangerous if ingested by a human being. The ingestion can be from eating contaminated food, breathing in radioactive dust, or drinking contaminated water. Alpha particles can't penetrate the skin, and beta particles can't penetrate heavy clothing. Thus if you are under cover, they are relatively harmless.

Gamma rays are somewhat akin to X-rays. They are highly penetrative and extremely dangerous to living tissue. Depending upon the intensity and the length of exposure to gamma rays, short-term results range from the negligible through incapacitating to death within twenty-four hours. The intensity of gamma-ray radiation is measured in Roentgen units, usually indicated by a numeral followed by the letter "R." For example, an intensity of 100 R shows that at a particular time and place, you will absorb one hundred units of radiation in a one-hour period. There are other systems in use, such as rads (Roentgen-absorbed doses) used for plants and the like and rems (Roentgen equivalent in man). However, all are somewhat similar. So if you have one hundred of one, you are likely to have pretty close to one hundred of the others.

Immediate radiation levels

Weapon yield	Radiation at 1 mile/1.6 Km	Radiation at 2 miles/3.2 Km	Radiation at 3 miles/4.8 Km
10 KT	80 R	100 mR	0.3 mR
20 KT	160 R	200 mR	0.6 mR
50 KT	440 R	550 mR	1.6 mR
100 KT	1,000 R	1.25 R	3.7 mR
200 KT	2,400 R	3.0 R	9.0 mR
500 KT	8,000 R	10.0 R	30.0 mR
1 MT	16,800 R	21.0 R	63.0 mR
10 MT	400,000 R	500.0 R	1.5 R

Note: 1 mR = 1 milliRoengten = 1/1,000th of a Roentgen.

Regrettably, radiation effects are cumulative in the human body. That is to say if you are exposed to 10 R today and another 10 R in a day or so, this will result in a 20-R exposure level, not 10 R. Too high an exposure will result in radiation sickness. A high initial exposure results in almost immediate incapacitation, while the same level of exposure over an extended period has a somewhat less serious consequence. The following table shows what to expect from exposure to various levels of radioactivity during a single twenty-four hour period.

Radiation Dosage (24-hour period)	Immediate Effect
100 R-150 R	Possibly some slight physical incapacitation depending upon the individual.
150 R-250 R	Nausea and vomiting within 24 hours; minor incapacitation after 48 hours.
250 R-350 R	Nausea and vomiting after 4 hours. Symptomatic remission from about the third day to the fourteenth day following exposure. Most people are incapacitated to some degree after that.
350 R-600 R	Immediate nausea and vomiting. Death within seven days. Higher levels of exposure result in faster death.

Again, if you have survived the initial blast and heat of a nuclear explosion, some intelligent preplanning will enable you to survive the subsequent fallout radiation, also. The rads accumulated in the first week are the critical ones and are the ones used in most examples dealing with survival.

Fortunately the level of radioactivity following a nuclear detonation does not remain constant. The radioactive decay principle shows that from a typical nuclear explosion, the decay rate is relatively rapid. For example, if the intensity at ground zero immediately after the detonation is 1,000 R after seven hours this will have decreased to 100 R. Then after seven of these seven-hour periods (forty-nine hours), the level of intensity will have fallen to 10 R. Two weeks later (forty-nine hours times seven), the level will be down to 1 R. This is known as the rule of seven.

The amount of internal damage sustained depends on several factors: the chemical nature of the radioisotope, the type of radiation emitted, the intensity of the radiation, radioactive half-life of the particle, the time it takes for the body to excrete half of the radioactive particle, called the biological half-life, and the amount in the body and its location.

Note: The time it takes for half of the isotope to break down is called its half-life. For example, carbon-14 takes 5,730 years, radon-222 takes 3.82 days, and uranium-238 takes 4.5 billion years.

This is not something that can be determined under disaster conditions. The tables below will, however, help.

Accumulated dosage within 21 hours–one-megaton nuclear device

	Cross and upwind			Downwind		
Dose rate	1,000 R/hr	300 R/hr	100 R/hr	1000 R/hr	300 R/hr	100 R/hr
Effect in one hour	lethal	border-line	asympto-matic	lethal	border-line	asympto-matic
1 hour	2 miles	8 miles	12 miles	20 miles	22 miles	22 miles
7 hours	8 miles	10 miles	18 miles	65 miles	80 miles	90 miles
21 hours	8 miles	12 miles	20 miles	100 miles	140 miles	180 miles

There are two special cases pertaining to radioactive decay. The first applies when nuclear missiles are intercepted and downed without exploding the warheads. The highly radioactive plutonium or uranium-238 will be strewn over the area of interception resulting in contaminated soil for thousands of years.

The second case pertains to nuclear power plants. These if targeted would not explode as a bomb would, however, their radioactive fuel would still be dispersed over a wide area, and the rate of decay is much slower. If you find that the rate of decay does not follow the rule of seven, you should consider moving out of the area as soon as the level of intensity drops to the 1-R level. It has been postulated that attack on a single nuclear power generation reactor with a single missile could devastate a substantial part of the eastern seaboard or Western Europe. A year after the attack, the 10 rems per-year-dose would still cover much of the area.

The incidence of radiation sickness would be very high following the use of nuclear weapons. Some knowledge of the symptoms will prove to be of value. The symptoms themselves are constant differing only in severity and they make their appearance depending on how much time elapsed since the initial exposure. This provides you with a rough idea whether the affected person has a possible chance of recovery.

For example, an initial exposure resulting in the absorption of 400 R within a one-hour period will result in the onset of nausea and vomiting occurring within three hours of the exposure. This is the first symptom, the duration of which will depend upon such variables as age, physical condition, and so on. This will be followed by a period of relative incapacity for work or movement, but with little actual pain or discomfort. This intermediate stage will last for about two weeks until the internal and progressive tissue damage caused by the radiation results in the manifestation of further external symptoms.

After about the second week, there will be increased internal hemorrhaging as the various organs commence to break down at the cellular level and the extensive and characteristic "bruising" caused by subcutaneous bleeding occurs. Patches of hair will fall out, and the individual generally feels sick and feverish.

After the third week, the person's condition will deteriorate further. Inflammation of the mouth and throat will become apparent. There will be severe diarrhea, accompanied by substantial weight loss. This will result in an emaciated appearance. The inflammation of the mouth and throat will worsen resulting in ulceration, which will gradually spread throughout the gastrointestinal tract. The terminal stage has now been reached, and the symptoms will increase in both severity and extent until the individual dies during the fourth week following exposure. Not a nice way to go.

So radiation sickness coupled with malnutrition, infected wounds, and a poor psychological state will be the principal cause of death and sickness in the first month after a nuclear explosion. The death toll will rise in the following months as lack of medical facilities denies treatment to people with wounds and sickness.

Radiation effects on normal tissue

Hematopoietic	Injury to the bone marrow may cause diminished production of blood elements
Cardiovascular	Pericarditis, inflammation of the sac surrounding the heart
Gonads • Males	200-300 rads, aspermatogensis, temporary halt of sperm production. 600-800 rads, sterility

Gonads • Females	200-300 rads, halt of menses 500-800 rads, permanent cessation of menses
Respiratory	Radiation pneumonia
Mouth, esophagus	Inflammation of mucus membranes with edema and painful swallowing of food may occur within hours or days after the onset of radiation

L-Cysteine will limit the damage of ionizing radiation if taken before exposure.

Not only do different parts of the body show different sensitivities to ionizing reactions, there are also variations in degrees of sensitivity among individuals. Generally, the faster a particular cell reproduces, the more vulnerable it is to radiation.

The effects of radiation on the human fetus are not fully known. However, it is known that the fetus is between twenty to sixty times more sensitive to radiation than a normal adult. Exposure to relatively low levels of radiation during pregnancy may result in the following deformities:

Stages of pregnancy	Anticipated deformity
20-54 days	Deformity of the fingers
25 days	Deafness
29 days	Curvature of the spine, microcephaly (dwarf head)
37 days	Skeletal deformity
41-70 days	Anemia

The long-term results upon the human race are likely to be even-more drastic as damaged and altered genes produce mutations for perhaps generations. In Japan following the bombing of Hiroshima and Nagasaki, spontaneous abortions and the production of monsters was common for decades afterward. So in the event of a nuclear war, racial heritage will no doubt be affected by deviations from our accepted norm. It is possible that similar results will also take place at all levels in the animal and vegetable world.

In this respect, the survival of domestic animals, wild game, and fish depends upon the extent and intensity of the radioactivity to which they were exposed. Regrettably, their tolerance is similar to that of mankind with dogs at the lower end of the scale and rats at the upper. The variables affecting the survival and future reproduction of both wild and domestic birds, as well as animals and fish, are so many that it is impossible to even guess at their future potential as a food source in the postdisaster period.

Certain areas may receive very little fallout enabling animal life in the area to survive with relative ease. If the attack comes in the winter months, the hibernating animals, such as bear, may survive in their dens. Beaver may be sufficiently protected by their environment. Muskrats and other burrowing animals may escape the consequences of fallout entirely, while animals subjected to relatively minor exposure may overcome the radiation sickness such exposure induces.

Fish, particularly those residing in the oceans, major inland bodies of water such as the Great Lakes, and fast-moving rivers and streams, are most likely to survive. They may, indeed, provide survivors with their major food source for a considerable time. Fish in relatively small lakes and ponds may be affected more seriously since these small, still bodies of water do not have the same self-cleansing properties as larger and more mobile bodies of water. The greatest danger to fish will be through the food chain. Algae and surface insects on which the smaller fish subsist may be heavily contaminated. The contamination will be passed on to the larger species as larger fish eat smaller fish and so on. Winter will provide the best protection for this food resource, particularly in the far north. There the depth of ice will provide almost 100-percent protection and levels of intensity will have dropped dramatically by the spring.

All in all, the possibilities of at least limited survival for fish and animals are quite good. Obviously, weak or sick animals, both wild and domestic, should not be used for food, and all should be checked for radioactivity with your detection gear.

Ionizing radiation affects all living tissue. Whether the cells are in vegetables or animals, they are sensitive to and are damaged by high levels of radiation. However, plants and animals vary widely in their sensitivity. A method known as Lethal Dose 50 percent, or LD_{50}, means that taken as an average, the sensitivity of an animal species to radiation is expressed as that dose which is lethal to 50 percent of that species.

LD$_{50}$ of various animals exposed to hard X-ray dosages
(in Roentgens)

Guinea pig	200-400 R
Swine	275 R
Dog	325 R
Goat	350 R
Monkey	500 R
Mouse	400-600 R
Rat	600-700 R
Hamster	700 R
Rabbit	800 R

Plant life may suffer from another side effect of a major nuclear confrontation. This is called a nuclear winter. Many studies suggest that with all the debris in the atmosphere, the sun's rays will be reflected away from the earth resulting in much-colder seasons. There is historical evidence for this. Major volcanic activity in the 1815 Tambora eruption in Indonesia was followed by a year with "no summer."

Intelligent preparation to survive the effects of radioactivity requires that in the first instance you have provided shelter capable of shielding the occupants from the immediate high radiation levels following a nuclear explosion. Secondly you must be able to measure not only the radiation levels, but also the accumulated radiation to which you have been exposed.

Intensity is measured directly in Roentgen units or sometimes in milliRoentgen units. Both scales are present in some measuring instruments, usually on the same dial, and the radiation being checked may even produce an audible "chatter," depending upon the instrument selected. Some radiation detection meters are available on the surplus market while the civilian version is the Geiger counter.

Personal accumulated dosage is recorded by a device known as a dosimeter, which should be worn constantly. The dosimeter provides a visual record of the amount of exposure the wearer has been exposed to expressed in Roentgen units. Dosimeters, when available, can be recalibrated to zero, usually by means of a "charger." Dosimeters are of different shapes and sizes. The most common one is shaped like a pen and carried the same way, except at waist level. There are film badges that serve

> *If you and your family anticipate surviving a nuclear experience, then every member must be in possession of a personal dosimeter.*

the same purpose. However, as they require specialized equipment to process, we do not recommend them for the survivor.

If you and your family anticipate surviving a nuclear experience, then every member must be in possession of a personal dosimeter. The group itself should have at least one radiacmeter or Geiger counter along with batteries or charging devices required to keep them functioning. These are still available from surplus outlets and stores specializing in survival supplies.

An electrostatic device is used to charge dosimeters. Some are powered by a single battery, while others are manual and thus rechargeable under field conditions.

The Kearny fallout meter is designed to be a homemade contraption. It was designed at the Oak Ridge National Laboratory. Dean Ing's *Pulling Through* science-fiction book had a copy of the contraption and how to build it. It was published by Ace Science Fiction in 1983, and you can find copies in secondhand bookstores. This is not a device to be made when the bombs are falling. The construction requires some practice beforehand.

In nature, the purple spiderwort stamen hairs change from blue to pink when exposed to as little as 150 millirems of radiation. This wildflower blooms April through July and is found on the prairies and in open woods, thickets, and meadows. By counting the number of cells changed in a hair, scientists can index the severity of radiation exposure.

Electromagnetic pulse (EMP)

Most experts agree that a full-scale nuclear attack would be initiated by a high-altitude (approximately two hundred miles high) nuclear explosion and that it would most probably be deployed from a satellite. A nuclear bomb detonated at that altitude will not have any significant damage on the earth's surface nor will it produce any significant radiation. The purpose of this explosion would be to damage critical electrical and electronic circuits in our weapons and communications capability. Only one such explosion could affect an area of a thousand miles in diameter.

Although the EMP release is only 1/100th that of the thermal radiation, it has a major effect on communications and electronics. Before the fireball phase, EMP is produced. The EMP pulse region overlaps much of the frequency spectrum. It is of very short duration, but emits its energy in the same portion of the spectrum as radio, TV, and radar frequencies.

Initially, it was thought that all vehicle electronic ignition and IC circuits would be fried. This is wrong. Modern vehicles having metal bodies are like Faraday boxes, and only vehicles with fiberglass bodies are susceptible to damage from a surge in EMP.

There is still a controversy pertaining to the EMP effect. We will follow the Defense Nuclear Agency's position in regard to EMP. It is formed either during a surface or near-surface burst or during a high-altitude air burst. Some overrated the EMP effect by stating that a single high-altitude burst would fry all our computers, radios, telephone switching centers, and other electronic equipment. What we know is that collectors, such as long runs of cable, house wiring, conduit, large antennas, overhead power and telephone lines, railroad tracks, etc., gather this energy in the form of a strong current and voltage surge. All solid-state electronic devices are vulnerable to this energy surge.

The equipment does not have to be attached directly to the collector in order to be damaged. It's possible for a collector to gather in the order of a joule of energy from a one-megaton, high-altitude explosion. It's estimated that the power grid throughout the United States will fail.

The power of the electromagnetic pulse is measured in microvolts per meter. Most radios are designed to receive wave pulses in the 1/10 microvolt range. Radio communication stations may have 10 v/m and a radar station may have as much as 200 v/m. In contrast the EMP at the blast site is 100,000 v/m, and even thirteen miles away, it will be in the area of 1,000 v/m.

We have two kinds of EMP damage. From a ground burst, we have a burnout of communication equipment and from an air burst, the temporary disruption due to the atmospheric ionization effect. Both would interrupt communication and electrical equipment. It is estimated the large-scale erasure of computer memories would accompany even this temporary disruption.

Radiological-measuring devices will not be affected by EMP, but EMP is capable of burning out radio transmitters, receivers, and transistors, and playing havoc with magnetic tapes. Short-lead radios, CB transmitters/receivers, and radios using loop antennas are deemed to be safe, while straight antenna receivers with less than a forty-inch lead are also thought to be safe.

At risk will be base stations, telephone systems, power-transmission lines, and anything with transistors. In general, if nuclear attack is expected, do the following:

- Disconnect computers, radio transmitters (actually unhook them from the antenna system), and store these in metal boxes. If no metal boxes are available, an old freezer will do if you wrap them in aluminum foil. Try to ground the Faraday box, moist earth is just fine. Faraday boxes piled on top of each other will ground as their metal covered sides will carry EMP to the ground.

- Disconnect all appliances from the electric grid.

- Harden antennas and the like by having double grounding systems.

I sincerely hope that information in this chapter will never be needed. Our civilization is extremely complex, and a nuclear bomb would be like a bucket of sand thrown into a fine wristwatch.

9
PREPARATIONS AT HOME

Emergency situations happen because we are not prepared. This lack of preparation makes it easy for a determined group to wreak havoc on us. Hurricanes are annual events in Florida. Yet after each warning, there is a general rush to get emergency supplies. Why? Because our memory seems to be very short when it comes to dealing with disaster. The same applies to surviving terrorists.

When you hear of increased terrorist activities following an international incident, then you should try to terrorist-proof your home, vehicle, and workplace. The precautions do not have to be so restricting that you become a prisoner in your home. But if you happily continue as you live today, you may be inviting an unplanned kidnaping or other terrorist act.

When one discusses preparations with people, most expect advice like purchasing riot shotguns, digging trenches in the front lawn, and buying gas masks. There is much surprise when I suggest having at least three days worth of supplies on hand. Why? Just look at any natural disaster, and you will find people risking their lives to buy spare batteries, infant formula, bread, and the like. During an ice storm that hit northern New York and parts of eastern Canada, many of the vehicles involved in accidents or sliding off the highway were driven by people trying to get supplies. In some places, the power was out for as many as eighteen days.

What to do:

1. Take a defensive-driving course.

2. Do not drive by yourself.

3. You can make good money by purchasing shares in companies manufacturing surveillance and security equipment.

4. It is best to conduct your affairs as if a terrorist incident could happen to you. Keep your eyes open for people following you, strangers in your neighborhood, and other unusual events.

5. Make sure that your permits and documents are up to date. Law enforcement is likely to be very rigorous.

6. Install a home security system.

7. Have a safe room in your house with a steel door, a telephone line in the room or a cellular phone, and some ready-to-eat food and water.

8. Keep abreast of local and international news.

9. Have a bug-out kit.

10. Review the identification you carry with you. It may be prudent to leave at home your twenty-year-old Marine Corps sharpshooting certificate and other similar identification papers.

11. Conduct a potential target evaluation. Know in which countries your employer operates.

12. I know it sounds dated, but fly El Al, the Israeli airline, if you can. Its preflight and in-flight security is unmatched.

13. Avoid large gatherings if you can. Any well-advertised event may also attract unwelcome attention by terrorists.

14. Do not use self-storage lockers. Close out any you may have. There are other storage options, such as private garage rentals.

15. If the terrorist activities continue, try to work from your home. This will eliminate much commuting and reduce your chances of being an unwitting target.

16. Take a good look at the ethnic makeup of your neighborhood. If you find that a large number of people are nationals of the country conducting the terrorist raids, you may want to move or increase your insurance coverage.

17. Listen to shortwave broadcasts coming from the country exporting the terrorists. Find out if they have any specific cities or events they may want to target.

18. Review your investments. If any of the companies you own stocks in have assets in the target countries, it may be time to sell them.

19. Invest in security-related stocks.

20. Find out which items are imported from the country behind the attacks. It may prove profitable to stock up on those items. This has to done in a logical fashion—Iranian rugs are not all that popular nowadays.

You do not need freeze-dried food. Ordinary canned goods such as you would normally eat are fine as long as they do not freeze. Just have more on hand, and rotate them so they don't go stale. I'm a firm believer in solar-charged appliances, including battery chargers. This way rather than having to run around trying to get batteries, you can sit at home and watch the situation unfolding. That is very important, particularly if you are a member of a visible minority group. The security elements will be on a heightened state of alert and will act decisively when faced with what they may perceive as a threat. By day three, a certain amount of normalcy will return, as we saw after the September 11 terrorist acts.

The first response of security elements after a terrorist incident is to set up roadblocks, search vehicles, and pay close attention to those behaving oddly. Woe to an eccentric or someone dressed in military-surplus clothing. They are likely to be detained, questioned, and have their identity verified. If you are wanted in a distant state for even a minor crime, you should be prepared to stay a guest of the state until things are sorted out. Under the proposed antiterrorist laws, if you are not a citizen, the incarceration will last longer. This is another example of why it pays to stay put until the situation calms down.

The problem with security forces, as demonstrated by September 11, is that they do not know whom to watch. However, after the event, they can quickly identify the perpetrators or the group sponsoring them. This twenty-twenty rear vision results in frustration, and the forces are likely to overreact when faced with people who look like the perpetrators. Listen to your media, and if you look like one of the terrorists, stay indoors and lay low. If the terrorist act has religious overtones, you may want to stay away from your place of worship. It could be closely monitored.

There are times when you must evacuate. Prepare in advance a small bug-out kit. The contents of mine are:

- flashlight and extra batteries;

- small multiband radio and extra batteries;

- plastic bags, these are useful for storing water;

- lighter or matches;

- comfort food, something you can eat without preparation, like chocolate bars;

- Swiss Army knife or a multitool;

- maps of your area and a compass;

- an emergency blanket available at most camping stores.

I know this does not sound like much, but it's easy to carry, so it will be with you when the unexpected happens. Many stores sell gadgets that may seem like a good thing to have, such as a small oxygen container and a mask to escape a smoke-filled area in case of a fire. Over the years, I tested many of these devices and concluded that an extra pair of shoes and a flashlight (with a working battery!) under the bed are more important.

Always have extra cash on hand. The first casualty of any disaster is loss of power. The ATM will not work and neither will the fuel pumps of most service stations. Keep your vehicle's gas tank at least half full at all times. From time to time, most of us forget these basic rules, and the results can be tragic. In a long life, I found that whenever I was ready for a storm or other event, it never happened. This can be said of terrorism, as well.

September 11 demonstrated that terrorists like to strike at unprepared targets. Can you imagine the outcome if the pilots were armed? At any rate, no amount of hand wringing will bring the dead to life. Now that we are prepared for hijacking of planes, our opponents will strike at something else. We do not know what the next target is, but we must be ready to react and protect ourselves and our families. Enough preaching.

One of the most important preparations is your mental attitude. If you read about any war, what emerges is that military units and even nations with the attitude of can-do and "We don't give up" prevailed over the enemy. Think of the passengers on the jet flying over Pennsylvania. In their attempt to overpower the hijackers, they lost their lives, but saved many other lives at the intended target location.

You can live in a fortress with five tons of supplies, but if you are not prepared to defend it, you might as well paint "Target" on the back of your shirt. I do not suggest for one minute that you cultivate the tough-guy image, just remember to reread Rudyard Kipling's poem "If" at least once a year. That should provide the essentials of mental preparedness.

10
PREPARATIONS AT THE WORKPLACE

The key to preparedness while traveling or working is to have emergency supplies with you. The large Magnalite at home is of no use if you are in the dark stairwell of a building. For example, on my key chain, I have a small AAA cell light and a tiny Swiss Army knife with a small blade, scissors, and nail file. Not exactly a multitool but it's always with me. I use one or the other at least three times a week. It is also useful to have a pair of walking boots at work and another pair in the trunk of the car.

Do you work for the government, a gynecologist, an embassy, or a religious organization? If so, you may be an unwitting target for terrorists. In this chapter, we must focus on two major issues. The first is safety in the workplace, and the second is how to get there and back. Oh yes, and then there are the letter bombs and anthrax. It is getting to the point where you can't open any mail coming from an unknown source.

If you are an American traveling in foreign lands, you must be careful. How careful? Careful enough to carry two wallets, one to give to the hijackers of your plane or your kidnaper. The "giveaway" wallet should have your driver's license, your library card, and like items. Your second wallet should contain your armed forces or government employee identification card, or any other documentation that would select you out for special treatment by your captors. This is just the first precaution you must take.

The standard advice given to potential targets is to avoid having a routine. This applies to the route you take to work as well as to your time of leaving home and arriving at your workplace. However, you should go beyond that. You have to establish "cutouts." What are cutouts? To give you an example, let me describe the daily activities of an acquaintance working for a target company in an unstable country.

He wakes up in the morning in a house rented by his girlfriend. After breakfast, she drives him in her minivan to an address in town where she backs the minivan into a garage. He gets out of the van and, using the back door, goes through a backyard and enters another backyard. He uses the remote starter for his car, which also opens the garage next door, waits four to five minutes, then unlocks his car door. A young man drives his car out of the garage, and he takes over while the young man drives ahead of him on his motorcycle. At the end of the day, he drives to a restaurant, and after leaving through the side door, a friend picks him up while the young man takes his car and drives it to his official residence.

Sounds like a lot of bother? It is, but he is still unhurt after five years in that country while many of his coworkers have been hurt, killed, kidnaped, or harassed on a daily basis. Use your imagination and dream up a host of others. The poor man's cutout will have to be less elaborate, but it can be done. Let us look at how. There is no set procedure for cutouts. However, we can look upon the major intelligence agencies' use of safe houses, creation of alternate identities, and travel techniques to provide examples of how to go about it.

When terrorist actions are taken against highly visible targets, the use of the above methods would be useful. As news of the terrorist action spreads, there will be copycats and want-to-bes who may come after you. In most countries today, people are living in a heightened state of alert.

Now that terrorist activities have escalated, people are kidnaped, murdered, and harmed by factions. If this continues, intolerance reaches the point of systemic violence. This can occur between antiabortion and pro-choice groups, big business and big unions, or what have you. When the level of violence increases, all those having business with or working for one of these organizations must take precautionary measures. Keep in mind that the police cannot protect you or your family around the clock.

Your employer may offer you and fellow workers a minibus service to pick you up, take you to work, and return you home. This supposed security measure will do nothing but provide a larger number of targets to a dedicated terrorist. It's better to make your own transportation arrangements because large organizations usually suffer from lack of imagination.

As the attacks become organized with pitched battles against security forces, they may even take the form of a guerrilla war. Spectacular hostage situations will arise like the one at the Japanese ambassador's residence in Lima, Peru. If you have to attend public functions, be extra careful. Have extra clothing in your vehicle, or even better, arrive in a small car wearing everyday clothes. To combat this, new regulations will be introduced to reduce public gatherings and ban protests. Some streets may be closed to vehicular traffic.

Some neighborhoods known to be home to target individuals will be selected for arson, drive-by shootings, and other terrorist acts.

About this time, you may decide to sleep where you work, or you may want to work out of your home. Random attacks on expensive cars may become routine during this phase. Some neighborhoods known to be home to target individuals will be selected for arson, drive-by shootings, and other terrorist acts.

Many affluent neighborhoods will become "gated" communities. That is, private security will control entry and patrol these areas. Gated communities will be relatively safe from random acts of violence, but will not be able to withstand an organized raid. They are at best a tripwire buying you time.

If the attacks are large scale, you may want to leave the country. This is particularly important if you look different from the local population. The various security agencies will add to the general confusion as there will be turf fights between them. This will further reduce the protection where it is most needed.

If the attacks continue, you may want to find another line of work or have a residence compound at work. You must balance the desirability of keeping your job with the risk inherent in keeping it. At a certain point, it's just not worth the hassle. You must be the judge of this.

The attacks may go well beyond targeting individuals who work for targets. It may extend to making hostages of the families of the employees and even their friends. Once this starts, you must revise your safety plans.

When the situation deteriorates to the point of a civil war, the government will have control. If you are faced with a civil war, leave. A polarization between factions has an unfortunate side effect of labeling people. Once you are so identified, you have very little chance of changing the label.

11
THE FIX TO THE SYSTEM

I n the final analysis, there will always be groups of people who are so determined to change the course of history that they will use any means to do so. What we need is a system of international cooperation to curtail these activities. Whether we succeed remains to be seen. The lifeblood of terrorism is money. With money, arms, supplies, and protection can be bought.

Somewhat hastily, Western nations made belated efforts to stop the flow of money to terrorists. Most of these efforts revolved around freezing the assets of suspected groups and individuals. Compared to bankers, the lemmings are freethinkers. Many, if not most, terrorist groups earn money from the drug-trafficking business. We will have to undertake a drastic rethinking about legalizing drugs and thereby cutting off the source of revenue for these groups. Once cut off, there is not much to seize. The terrorists would have to sell chocolate bars from tent to tent or have bottle drives just to buy ammunition with which to train.

There is not much sense in revisiting eight-hundred-year old injustices. We have to live with the world as it is. The American desire to retire to "fortress North America" is pointless until we cut our dependency on foreign oil. This means rethinking and reshaping our energy policy. The only time we will be free of foreign entanglements is when we have energy self-sufficiency. This requires a whole new investment in alternate sources of energy and propulsion such as fuel cells. Isolation and decoupling from world affairs is impossible until this is achieved. And even then we must keep in mind that Uncle Sam is a global trader, notwithstanding wishful thinking.

> *In Israel, about 10 percent of the adult population possesses concealed-carry permits, and during high alerts, the authorities urge all of them to carry their handguns.*

The director of homeland security should look to the example of Israel. In that country, terrorists bent on killing civilians usually wait until police and military personnel leave the area to begin killing. Their first targets are those carrying assault rifles and submachine guns. Like in our country, there are many people with concealed carry permits. These are the people who are the last line of defense to reduce the toll of casualties in a terrorist attack. In Israel, about 10 percent of the adult population possesses concealed-carry permits, and during high alerts, the authorities urge all of them to carry their handguns.

We are not much of a democracy if we do not trust our citizens to be armed. So rather than limiting the practice to thirty-three states, we should allow concealed-carry laws in all states of the union. Imagine the surprise of a group of terrorists attempting the hijack of an airliner. Here, as in Israel, we know that the police and military can't be everywhere. So we should let our citizens provide enhanced security for the nation.

In the last ten years or so, guns have been demonized. This is wrong. We should remember the doggerel engraved upon the grip of one of Sam Colt's revolvers:

> *Be not afraid of any man*
> *no matter what his size*
> *When danger threatens, call on me*
> *and I will equalize*

That is as true today as it was at the turn of the twentieth century. We should once again look on firearms as specialized tools, nothing more, nothing less. Unless I get safety instruction in the use of a chain saw, I would not use one. This should apply to firearms, as well.

In regards to our intelligence efforts, we must refocus on HUMINT. That is human intelligence, meaning that we must have people in various countries who can provide information on what is happening. We are so focused on the "glass eye," meaning satellites, photo intelligence, and other high-tech devices, that we can be defeated by a $1.47 emergency blanket. How? If you have a person under one of these blankets all the infrared imaging won't show any "hot spots."

To improve on human intelligence, we have to recruit informers as we have done during the Cold War days. The CIA prefers computers to unreliable people in some godforsaken corner of the globe. However, if a terrorist plan is hatched and a person or persons then carry it out elsewhere, all the high-tech information-gathering systems are of no use. This is where the informer in the terrorist organization pays off. Once again, Israel provides an example on how to do this.

At one point, by presidential order, no one with a criminal background was employed by the intelligence agencies. The fundamental tenet of police operations was ignored, "to catch a thief, you set a thief." We should take lessons from countries that seem to be able to counter terrorists. The other facet of change should be better cooperation between national agencies. Many of the agencies jealously guard the information they collect. As a result, until all information is collected, we only have part of the picture of a plan directed at harming us.

We should study the history and customs of other countries, in particular those who are demonized by the media today. What will this provide? A general understanding of the grievances these countries have against us. With a little knowledge, instead of sending bombers, perhaps we could send them computers for their schools. America is a magnet for professionals from all over the world. This applies to training as well as working here.

We could use foreign aid to subsidize the wages of these professionals so that they can help their countrymen. This is not liberal wishful thinking. Consider this. How many dictators would support an attack on America if as a result they could lose one-half of their health-care services? Would the people of Indonesia demonstrate against American "imperialism" if the health clinics were staffed by American-trained doctors?

It's in our national self-interest to not just help, but also be viewed as acting in the best interest of other countries. There will always be people who think of America as the "Great Satan." They will not have safe havens if others realize that this is not so. What will make the difference is how we are perceived by the "common people" in other lands.

The head offices of most of the multinational companies are in the U.S. There is general resentment against many of these companies, and in turn, this resentment is directed against America. If one reads the history of

United Fruit, the plight of many Central American countries becomes clearer. When corrupt governments and dictators are supported in aid of multinational companies, we create potential terrorists.

APPENDIX: PROFILES OF TERRORIST ORGANIZATIONS

T he following list of terrorist groups is not exhaustive. It includes the major groups that have been active recently, but does not include those whose activities have been more limited in scope.

ABU NIDAL ORGANIZATION (ANO)

a.k.a. Fatah Revolutionary Council, Arab Revolutionary Brigades, Black September, and Revolutionary Organization of Socialist Muslims

Description: An international terrorist organization led by Sabri al-Banna. Split from PLO in 1974. Made up of various functional committees, including political, military, and financial.

Activities: Has carried out terrorist attacks in twenty countries, killing or injuring nine hundred people. Targets include the United States, the United Kingdom, France, Israel, moderate Palestinians, the PLO, and various Arab countries. Major attacks included the Rome and Vienna airports in 1985, the Neve Shalom synagogue in Istanbul, Pan Am flight 73 hijacking in Karachi in September 1986, and the *City of Poros* day-excursion ship attack in July 1988 in Greece. Suspected of assassinating PLO deputy chief Abu

Hul in Tunis in January 1991. ANO assassinated a Jordanian diplomat in Lebanon in January 1994 and has been linked to the killing of the PLO representative there. Has not attacked Western targets since the late 1980s.

Strength: Several hundred plus militia in Lebanon and an overseas support structure.

Location/Area of operation: al-Banna relocated to Iraq in December 1998, where the group maintains a presence. Has operational bases in Lebanon in the al-Biqa's Bekaa Valley and several Palestinian refugee camps in coastal areas of Lebanon. Also has a presence in Sudan. Has demonstrated ability to operate over wide area, including the Middle East, Asia, and Europe. Libya and Egypt shut down ANO's operations in 1999.

External aid: Has received considerable support, including safe haven, training, logistic assistance, and financial aid from Iraq and Syria (until 1987). Continues to receive monetary aid from Libya, in addition to close support for selected operations.

ABU SAYYAF GROUP (ASG)

Description: Islamic extremist group operating in the southern Philippines. Split from the Moro National Liberation Front since 1991. With the death of Abdurajik Abubaker Janjalani in December 1998, it's reported that Khadafi Janjalani, his younger brother, is the new leader.

Activities: Uses bombs, assassinations, kidnaping for ransom, and extortion from companies and businessmen in its efforts to promote an Islamic state in Western Mindanao (an island in the southern Philippines heavily populated by Muslims) and the Sulu Archipelago. Staged a raid on the town of Ipil in Mindanao in April 1995, the group's first large-scale action. Kidnaped more than thirty foreigners, including a U.S. citizen, in 2000.

Strength: About 200 members, mostly younger Muslims, many of whom have studied or worked in the Gulf states, where they were exposed to radical Islamic ideology.

Location/Area of operation: The ASG operates in the southern Philippines and occasionally in Manila. Extended its area of operations to Malaysia in 2000 by abducting foreigners from two different resorts.

External aid: Probably has ties to Islamic extremists in the Middle East and South Asia.

AL-JIHAD (SEE UNDER J)

ALEX BONCAYAO BRIGADE (ABB)

Description: The ABB, the urban hit squad of the Communist Party of the Philippines New Peoples' Party was formed in the mid-1980s.

Activities: The ABB is responsible for more than one hundred murders and is believed to have been involved in the 1989 murder of U.S. Army Col. James Rowe in the Philippines. Although reportedly decimated by a series of arrests in late 1995, the June 1996 murder of a former high-ranking Philippine official, claimed by the group, demonstrates that it still maintains terrorist capabilities. In March 2000, the group claimed credit for a rifle grenade attack against the Department of Energy Building in Manila and strafed Shell Oil offices in the central Philippines to protest rising oil prices.

Strength: Approximately 500.

Location/Area of operation: Operates in Manila and central Philippines.

External aid: Unknown.

ARMED ISLAMIC GROUP (GIA)

Description: An Islamic extremist group, the GIA aims to overthrow the secular Algerian regime and replace it with an Islamic state. Began its violent activities in early 1992 after Algiers voided the victory of the Islamic Salvation Front (FIS)–the largest Islamic party–in the first round of the December 1991 legislative elections.

Activities: Frequent attacks against regime targets, particularly security personnel and government officials, also civilians, journalists, teachers, and foreign residents. Since announcing its terrorist campaign against foreigners living in Algeria in September 1993, the GIA has killed about one hundred expatriate men and women, mostly Europeans, in the country. The GIA uses assassinations and bombings, including car bombs, and is known to favor kidnaping victims and slitting their throats. The GIA hijacked an Air France flight to Algiers in December 1994, and suspicions centered on the group for a series of bombings in France in 1995 and again in late 1996.

The Salafi Group for Call and Combat (GSPC) splinter faction appears to have eclipsed the GIA since 1998.

Strength: Unknown, probably several hundred to several thousand.

Location/Area of operation: Algeria and France.

External aid: Algerian expatriates, many of whom reside in Western Europe, provide some financial and logistic support. In addition, the Algerian government has accused Iran and Sudan of supporting Algerian extremists and in March 1993, severed diplomatic relations with Iran.

ARMY FOR THE LIBERATION OF RWANDA
(ALIR, INTERAHAMWE, FORMER ARMED FORCES)

Description: The FAR was the army of the Rwandan Hutu regime that carried out the genocide of 500,000 or more Tutsis and regime opponents in 1994. The Interahamwe was the civilian militia force that carried out much of the killing. The groups merged after they were forced from Rwanda into the Democratic Republic of the Congo (then Zaire) in 1994.

Activities: The group seeks to topple Rwanda's Tutsi-dominated government, reinstate Hutu control, and possibly, complete the genocide. In 1999, ALIR guerrillas, critical of alleged U.S.-UK support for the Rwandan regime, kidnaped and killed eight foreign tourists, including two U.S. citizens, in a game park on the Congo-Uganda border. In the current Congolese war, the ALIR is allied with Kinshasa against the Rwandan invaders.

Strength: Several thousand ALIR regular forces operate alongside the Congolese army on the front lines of the Congo civil war, while a like number of ALIR guerrillas operate behind Rwanda lines in eastern Congo closer to the Rwandan border and sometimes within Rwanda.

Location/Area of operation: Mostly Democratic Republic of the Congo and Rwanda, but a few may operate in Burundi.

External Aid: From the Rwandan invasion of 1998 until his death in early 2001, the Laurent Kabila regime in the Democratic Republic of the Congo provided the ALIR with training, arms and supplies.

AUM SUPREME TRUTH (AUM)
AKA: AUM SHINRIKO

Description: A cult established in 1987 by Shoko Asahara, Aum aims to take over Japan and then the world. Its organizational structure mimics that of a nation-state, with "ministries" and a "pope secretariat." Followers are controlled by a mix of charisma and coercion. Approved as a religious entity in 1989 under Japanese law, the group was active in local Japanese elections in 1990. Disbanded as a religious organization under Japanese law in October 1995. In 2000, Fumihiro Joyu took control and changed the name to Aleph.

Activities: On March 20, 1995, Aum members carried six packages onto Tokyo subway trains and punctured the packages with umbrella tips, releasing deadly sarin nerve gas that killed twelve people and injured more than five thousand. Japanese police arrested Asahara in May 1995. Several key Aum figures remain at large. The group may have perpetrated other crimes before the March 1995 attack and apparently planned other attacks. The cult scaled back its activities in 2000.

Strength: At the time of the Tokyo subway attack, the group claimed to have 9,000 members in Japan and up to 40,000 worldwide. Its current strength is estimated between 1,500 to 2,000 people.

Location/Area of operation: In addition to Japan, the group has maintained a presence in Russia.

External aid: None.

BASQUE FATHERLAND AND LIBERTY (ETA)

Description: Founded in 1959 with the aim of creating an independent homeland based on Marxist principles in the northern Spanish provinces of Vizcaya, Guipuzcoa, Alava, and Navarra and the southwestern French provinces of Labourd, Basse-Navarre, and Soule.

Activities: Chiefly bombings and assassinations of Spanish government officials, especially security and military forces, as well as judicial figures. In response to French operations against the group, ETA has targeted French interests. It finances its activities through kidnaping, robbery, and extortion. In 1995 Spanish and French authorities foiled an ETA plot to kill King Juan Carlos in Majorca.

Strength: Unknown, may have hundreds of members, plus supporters.

Location/Area of operation: Operates primarily in the Basque autonomous regions of northern Spain and southwestern France, but has bombed Spanish and French interests elsewhere.

External aid: Has received training at various times in Libya, Lebanon, and Nicaragua. Also appears to have close ties to the Irish Republican Army (IRA) through the groups' political wing.

CHUKAKU-HA (NUCLEUS OR MIDDLE CORE FRACTION)

Description: An ultra-leftist/radical group with origins in the fragmentation of the Japanese Communist Party in 1957. One of the largest domestic militant groups; has political arm plus small, covert action wing called Kansai Revolutionary Army. Funding derived from membership dues, sales of its newspapers, and fund-raising campaigns.

Activities: Participates in street demonstrations and commits sporadic attacks using crude rockets and incendiary devices usually designed to cause property damage rather than casualties. Protests Japan's imperial system, Western imperialism, and events like the Gulf War and the expansion of Tokyo's Narita airport. Has launched rockets at a U.S. military facility.

Strength: 3,500.

Location/Area of operation: Japan.

External aid: None known.

DEMOCRATIC FRONT FOR THE LIBERATION OF PALESTINE (DFLP)

Description: Marxist group that split from the PFLP in 1969. Believes Palestinian national goals can be achieved only through revolution of the masses. Opposes the Declaration of Principles (DOP) signed in 1993. In the early 1980s, occupied political stance halfway between Arafat and the rejectionists. Split into two factions in 1991, one pro-Arafat and part of the PLO and another more hard-line faction headed by Nayef Hawatmeh, which has suspended participation in the PLO.

Activities: In the 1970s, carried out numerous small bombings and minor assaults and some spectacular operations in Israel and the occupied territories, concentrating on Israeli targets. Involved only in border raids since 1988, but continues to oppose the Israel-PLO peace agreement.

Strength: Estimated at 500 (total for both factions).

Location/Area of operation: Syria, Lebanon, and the Israeli-occupied territories of Palestine. Attacks have taken place entirely in Israel and occupied territories.

External aid: Receives financial and military aid from Syria and Libya.

DEVRIMCI SOL (REVOLUTIONARY LEFT) AKA: DEV SOL
*(see Revolutionary People's Liberation
Party/Front, DHKP/C)*

ELA
(see Revolutionary People's Struggle)

ELN
(see National Liberation Army)

ETA
(see Basque Fatherland and Liberty)

FARC
(see Revolutionary Armed Forces of Colombia)

FIRST OF OCTOBER ANTIFASCIST RESISTANCE GROUP
(GRAPO)

Description: Formed in 1975 as the armed wing of the illegal Communist Party of Spain of the Franco era. Advocates the overthrow of the Spanish government and replacing it with a Marxist-Leninist one. GRAPO is extremely anti-U.S. Calls for the removal of all American forces from Spanish territory.

Activities: GRAPO has killed more than eighty people and injured more than two hundred. In November 2000, GRAPO operatives shot to death a Spanish policeman in reprisal for the arrest in France of several group leaders.

Strength: Unknown, but likely fewer than a dozen hard-core activists.

Location/Area of operation: Spain.

External aid: None.

FPMR
(see Manuel Rodriguez Patriotic Front)

AL-GAMA'AT AL-ISLAMIYYA (ISLAMIC GROUP, IG)

Description: An indigenous Egyptian extremist group active since the late 1970s. Appears to be loosely organized. Led by Mustafa Hamza. Shekh Umar Abd al-Rahman is the preeminent spiritual leader. Goal is to over-throw the government of President Hosni Mubarak and replace it with an Islamic state.

Activities: Armed attacks against Egyptian security and other govern-ment officials, Coptic Christians, and Egyptian opponents of Islamic extremism. The group also has launched attacks on tourists in Egypt since 1992. Al-Gama'at claimed responsibility for the attempt in June 1995 to assassinate President Hosni Mubarak in Addis Ababa, Ethiopia. This group attacked foreign tourists at Luxor in November 1997 leaving more than sixty dead.

Strength: Not known, but probably several thousand hard-core members and several thousand sympathizers. This probably diminished after a 1998 cease-fire.

Location/Area of operation: Operates mainly in the al-Minya, Asyut, and Qina governorates of southern Egypt. It also appears to have support in Cairo, Alexandria, and other urban locations, particularly among unem-ployed graduates and students.

External aid: Not known. Egyptian government believes that Iran, bin

Laden, and Afghan militant Islamic groups supported them. That support is probably not available now.

HAMAS (ISLAMIC RESISTANCE MOVEMENT)

Description: HAMAS was formed in late 1987 as an outgrowth of the Palestinian branch of the Muslim brotherhood. Various elements of HAMAS have used both political and violent means, including terrorism, to pursue the goal of establishing an Islamic Palestinian state in place of Israel. HAMAS is loosely structured, with some elements working openly through mosques and social-service organizations to recruit members, raise money, organize activities, and distribute propaganda. Militant elements of HAMAS, operating clandestinely, have advocated and used violence to advance their goals. HAMAS' strength is concentrated in the Gaza Strip and a few areas of the West Bank. It has also engaged in peaceful political activity, such as running candidates in the West Bank Chamber of Commerce elections.

Activities: HAMAS activists, especially those in the Izz el-Din al Qassem Forces, have conducted many attacks against Israeli civilian and military targets, suspected Palestinian collaborators, and Fatah rivals. Claimed several attacks during the unrest in late 2000.

Strength: Unknown number of hard-core members; tens of thousands of supporters and sympathizers.

Location/Area of operation: Primarily the occupied territories and Israel. In 1999 Jordanian authorities closed the group's political bureau offices in Annam, arrested its leaders, and prohibited the group from operating on Jordanian territory.

External aid: Receives funding from Palestinian expatriates, Iran, and private benefactors in Saudi Arabia and other moderate Arab states. Some fund-raising and propaganda activity take place in Western Europe and North America.

THE HARAKAT UL-MUJAHIDIN
(HUM, HARAKAT UL-ANSAR, HUA)

Description: HUM, an Islamic militant group that is based in Pakistan and operates mainly in Kashmir, was formed in October 1993 when two

Pakistani political activist groups, Harakat ul-Jihad and Harakat ul-Mujahedin, merged. The leader Faruoq Kashmiri, like the previous leader, has close ties to bin Laden. Operates training camps in eastern Afghanistan.

Activities: Has carried out a number of operations against Indian troops and civilian targets in Kashmir. A HUM-associated hijacker captured an Indian airliner on December 24, 2000, and traded the passengers for Masood Azhar, who was jailed in India. Upon his release, Azhar did not rejoin the HUM, choosing the more radical Jaish-e-Mohammed group.

Strength: Has several thousand armed members located in Azad Kashmir, Pakistan, and in the southern Kashmir and the Doda regions of India. The HUA uses light and heavy machine guns, assault rifles, mortars, explosives, and rockets. Membership is open to all who support the HUA's objectives and are willing to take the group's forty-day training course. It has a core militant group of about three hundred, mostly Pakistanis and Kashmiris, but includes Afghans and Arab veterans of the Afghan war.

Location/Area of operation: The HUA is based in Muzaffarabad, Pakistan, but HUA members have participated in insurgent and terrorist operations in Kashmir, Myanmar (Burma), Tajikistan, and Bosnia and Herzegovina. The HUA is actively involved in supporting Muslims in Indian-controlled Kashmir with humanitarian and military assistance. The HUA's Burma branch, located in the Arakan Mountains, trains local Muslims in handling weapons and guerrilla warfare. In Tajikistan, HUA members have served with and trained Tajik resistance elements. The first group of Harakat militants entered Bosnia in 1992.

External aid: The HUA collects donations from Saudi Arabia and other Gulf and Islamic states to purchase relief supplies, which it distributes to Muslims in Tajikistan, Kashmir, and Burma. The source and amount of HUA's military funding are unknown, but are believed to come from sympathetic Arab countries and wealthy Pakistanis and Kashmiris.

HIZBALLAH (PARTY OF GOD)

aka: Islamic Jihad, Revolutionary Justice Organization, Organization of the Oppressed on Earth, and Islamic Jihad for the Liberation of Palestine

Description: Radical Shia group formed in Lebanon, dedicated to creation of Iranian-style Islamic republic in Lebanon and removal of all non-Islamic influences from the area. Strongly anti-West and anti-Israel. Closely allied with, and often directed by, Iran, but may have conducted rogue operations that were not approved by Tehran.

Activities: Known or suspected to have been involved in numerous anti-U.S. terrorist attacks, including the suicide truck bombing of the U.S. Embassy and U.S. Marine barracks in Beirut in October 1983 and the U.S. Embassy annex in Beirut in September 1984. Elements of the group were responsible for the kidnaping and detention of U.S. and other Western hostages in Lebanon. The group also attacked the Israeli Embassy in Argentina in 1992. In fall 2000, it captured three Israeli soldiers in the Shebaa Farms and kidnaped an Israeli noncombatant who may have been lured into Lebanon on false pretenses.

Strength: Several thousand supporters and a few hundred terrorist operatives.

Location/Area of operation: Operates in the Bekaa Valley, the southern suburbs of Beirut, and southern Lebanon. Has established cells in Europe, Africa, South America, North America, and elsewhere.

External aid: Receives substantial amounts of financial, training, weapons, explosives, political, diplomatic, and organizational aid from Iran and Syria.

IRISH REPUBLICAN ARMY (IRA)
aka: Provisional Irish Republican Army (PIRA), the Provos
Description: Radical terrorist group formed in 1969 as a clandestine armed wing of Sinn Fein, a legal political movement dedicated to removing British forces from Northern Ireland and unifying Ireland. Has a Marxist orientation. Organized into small, tightly knit cells under the leadership of the Army Council.

Activities: Bombings, assassinations, kidnapings, extortion, and robberies. Before its 1994 cease-fire, targets included senior British government officials, British military and police in Northern Ireland, and Northern Irish loyalist paramilitary groups. Since breaking its cease-fire in February 1996 IRA's operations have included bombing campaigns against train and subway stations and shopping areas on mainland Britain, British military and

APPENDIX

Royal Ulster Constabulary targets in Northern Ireland, and a British military facility on the European continent.

Strength: Several hundred, plus several thousand sympathizers.

Location/Area of operation: Northern Ireland, Irish Republic, Great Britain, and Europe.

External aid: Has received aid from a variety of groups and countries and considerable training and arms from Libya and, at one time, the PLO. Also is suspected of receiving funds and arms from sympathizers in the United States. Similarities in operations suggest links to ETA.

ISLAMIC MOVEMENT OF UZBEKISTAN (IMU)

Description: Coalition of Islamic militants from Uzbekistan and other Central Asian states opposed to Uzbeki President Islom Karimov's secular regime. Goal is establishment of Islamic state in Uzbekistan. Recent propaganda also includes anti-Western and anti-Israeli rhetoric.

Activities: Believed to be responsible for five car bombs in Tashkent in February 1999. Took hostages on several occasions in 1999 and 2000, including four U.S. citizens who were mountain climbing in August 2000, four Japanese geologists, and eight Kyrgyzstani soldiers in August 1999.

Strength: Militants probably number in the thousands.

Location/Area of operation: Militants are based in Afghanistan and Tajikistan. Area of operations includes Uzbekistan, Tajikistan, Kyrgyzstan, and Afghanistan.

External aid: Support from other Islamic extremist groups in Central and South Asia. IMU leadership broadcasts statements over Iranian radio.

ISLAMIC RESISTANCE MOVEMENT
(see HAMAS)

JAISH-E-MOHAMMED (JEM, ARMY OF MOHAMMED)

Description: JEM is an Islamist group based in Pakistan that has rapidly expanded in size and capability since Maulana Masood Azhar, a former fundamentalist Harakat ul-Ansar leader, formed it in 2000. The group's aim is to unite Kashmir with Pakistan. It is politically with the radical, pro-Taliban Jamiat-i Ulema-i Islam party. Some of the leaders were recently placed under arrest by Pakistani authorities.

Activities: In December 2000, JEM militants launched grenade attacks at a bus stop in Kupwara, India injuring sixteen people. Two bombs planted by JEM members killed twenty-one people in Qamarwari and Srinagar.

Strength: Has several hundred armed supporters located in Azad Kashmir, Pakistan, and India's southern Kashmir and Doda regions. Supporters are mostly Pakistanis and Kashmiris and also include Afghans and Arab veterans of the Afghan war. Uses light and heavy machine guns, assault rifles, mortars, improvised explosive devices, and rocket-propelled grenades.

Location/Area of operation: Based in Peshawar and Muzaffarabad, but members conduct terrorist activities primarily in Kashmir. JEM maintains training camps in Afghanistan. These camps are now closed down.

External aid: Most of the JEM's cadre and material resources have been drawn from the militant groups Harakat ul-Jihad and the Harakat ul-Mujahedin. JEM has close ties to Afghan Arabs and the Taliban. It is suspected that Osama bin Laden was funding JEM.

JAMAAT UL-FUQRA

Description: Jamaat ul-Fuqra is an Islamic sect that seeks to purify Islam through violence. Fuqra is led by Pakistani cleric Sheikh Mubarak Ali Gilani, who established the organization in the early 1980s. Gilani now resides in Pakistan, but most Fuqra cells are located in North America. Fuqra members have purchased isolated rural compounds in North America to live communally, practice their faith, and isolate themselves from Western culture. Recently the Pakistani government cracked down on their activities.

Activities: Fuqra members have attacked a variety of targets that they view as enemies of Islam, including Muslims they regard as heretics and Hindus. Attacks during the 1980s included assassinations and firebombings across the United States. Fuqra members in the United States have been convicted of criminal violations, including murder and fraud.

Strength: Unknown.

Location/Area of operation: North America, Pakistan.

External aid: None.

JAPANESE RED ARMY (JRA)
aka: Anti-Imperialist International Brigade (AIIB)

Description: An international terrorist group formed around 1970 after breaking away from Japanese Communist League-Red Army Faction. It was led by Fusako Shigenobu until her arrest in Japan. Stated goals are to overthrow the Japanese government and monarchy and to help foment world revolution. Organization unclear, but may control or at least have ties to Anti-imperialist International Brigade (AIIB). Details released following arrest in November 1987 of leader Osamu Maruoka indicate that JRA may have been organizing cells in Asian cities, such as Manila and Singapore. Has had close ties and longstanding relations with Palestinian terrorist groups, based and operating outside Japan, since its inception.

Activities: During the 1970s, JRA carried out a series of attacks around the world, including the massacre in 1972 at Lod airport in Israel, two Japanese airliner hijacks, and an attempted takeover of the U.S. Embassy in Kuala Lumpur. In April 1988, JRA operative Yu Kikumura was arrested carrying explosives on the New Jersey Turnpike, apparently planning an attack to coincide with the bombing of a USO club in Naples, a suspected JRA operation that killed five, including a U.S. servicewomen. He was convicted of these charges and is serving a lengthy prison sentence in the United States. Several other hard-core members have been arrested around the world in recent years. Some have been deported to Japan.

Strength: About six hard-core members, undetermined number of sympathizers.

Location/Area of operation: Based in Syrian-controlled areas of Lebanon, often seen in Damascus.

External aid: Unknown.

PROFILES OF TERRORIST ORGANIZATIONS

AL-JIHAD

aka: Jihad Group, Vanguards of Conquest, Talaa' al-Fateh, International Justice Group, World Justice Group

Description: An Egyptian Islamic extremist group active since the late 1970s. Appears to be divided into at least two separate functions: remnants of the original Jihad led by Abbud al-Zumar, currently imprisoned in Egypt, and a faction calling itself Vanguards of Conquest (Talaa' al-Fateh). The Vanguards of Conquest appear to be led by Dr. Ayman al-Zawahiri, who is currently outside of Egypt; his specific whereabouts are unknown. Like al-Gama'at al-Islamiyya, the Jihad factions regard Sheikh Umar Abd-al Rahman as their spiritual leader. The goal of all Jihad factions is to overthrow the government of President Hosni Mubarak and replace it with an Islamic state.

Activities: Specializes in armed attacks against high-level Egyptian government officials. The original Jihad was responsible for the assassination in 1981 of President Anwar Sadat. Unlike al-Gama'at al-Islamiyya, which largely targets mid- and lower-level security personnel, Coptic Christians, and Western tourists, al-Jihad appears to concentrate on high-level, high-profile Egyptian government officials, including cabinet ministers. Claimed responsibility for the attempted assassinations of Interior Minister Hassan al-Alfi in August 1993 and Prime Minister Atef Sedky in November 1993.

Strength: Not known, but probably several thousand hard-core members and another several thousand sympathizers among the various factions.

Location/Area of operation: Operates mainly in the Cairo area. Also appears to have members outside Egypt, mainly in Afghanistan, Pakistan, and Sudan.

External aid: Not known. The Egyptian government claims that Iran, Sudan, and militant Islamic groups in Afghanistan support the Jihad factions.

KACH AND KAHANE CHAI

Description: Stated goal is to restore the Biblical state of Israel. Kach (founded by radical Israeli-American rabbi Meir Kahane) and its offshoot, Kahane Chai, which means "Kahane lives," (founded by Meir Kahane's son, Binyamin, following his father's assassination in the United States) were declared to be terrorist organizations in March 1994 by the Israeli cabinet under the 1948 Terrorism Law. This followed the groups' statements in support of Dr. Baruch Goldstein's attack in February 1994 on the al-Ibrahimi Mosque. Goldstein was affiliated with Kach. They attack the Israeli government's peace process.

Activities: Organize protests against the Israeli government. Harass and threaten Palestinians in Hebron and the West Bank. Groups have threatened to attack Arabs, Palestinians, and Israeli government officials. They also claimed responsibility for several shooting attacks on West Bank Palestinians in which four people were killed and two were wounded in 1993.

Strength: Unknown.

Location/Area of operation: Israel and West Bank settlements, particularly Qiryat Arba' in Hebron.

External aid: Receives support from sympathizers in the United States and Europe.

KHMER ROUGE
(see Party of Democratic Kampuchea)

KURDISTAN WORKERS' PARTY (PKK)

Description: Established in 1974 as a Marxist-Leninist insurgent group primarily composed of Turkish Kurds. In recent years has moved beyond rural-based insurgent activities to include urban terrorism. Seeks to set up an independent Kurdish state in southeastern Turkey, where there is a predominantly Kurdish population. Turkish authorities captured Chairman Abdullah Ocalan in Kenya.

Activities: Primary targets are Turkish government security forces in Turkey, but also has been active in Western Europe against Turkish targets. Conducted attacks on Turkish diplomatic and commercial facilities in dozens of West European cities in 1993 and again in the spring of 1995. In an attempt to damage Turkey's tourism industry, the PKK has bombed tourist sites and hotels and kidnaped foreign tourists.

Strength: Approximately 5,000 to 10,000 guerrillas, mostly located in northern Iraq. Has thousands of sympathizers in Turkey and Europe.

Location/Area of operation: Operates in Turkey, Europe, the Middle East, and Asia.

External aid: Receives safe haven and modest aid from Syria, Iraq, and Iran.

LIBERATION TIGERS OF TAMIL EELAM (LTTE)

Description: Founded in 1976, the LTTE is the most-powerful Tamil group in Sri Lanka and uses overt and illegal methods to raise funds, acquire weapons, and publicize its cause of establishing an independent Tamil state. The LTTE began its armed conflict with the Sri Lankan government in 1983 and relies on a guerrilla strategy that includes the use of terrorist tactics. The movement has a number of front organizations. These are the World Tamil Association (WTA), World Tamil Movement (WTM), Federation of Associations of Canadian Tamils (FACT), the Ellalan Force, and the Sangillan Force.

Activities: The LTTE has integrated a battlefield insurgent strategy with a terrorist program that targets not only key personnel in the countryside, but also senior Sri Lankan political and military leaders in Colombo. Political assassinations have included former Indian Prime Minister Rajiv Gandhi in 1991 and President Ranasinghe Premadasa in 1993. The LTTE has refrained from targeting Western tourists, fearing that foreign governments would crack down on Tamil expatriates involved in fund-raising activities abroad.

Strength: Approximately 10,000 armed combatants in Sri Lanka; about 3,000 to 6,000 form a trained cadre of fighters. Also has a significant overseas support structure for fund-raising, weapons procurement, and propaganda activities.

Location/Area of operation: The LTTE controls most of the northern and eastern areas of Sri Lanka, but has conducted operations throughout the island. Headquartered in the Jaffna peninsula, LTTE leader Velupillai Prabhakaran has established an extensive network of checkpoints and informants to keep track of any outsiders who enter the group's area of control. The LTTE prefers to attack vulnerable government facilities, then withdraw before reinforcements arrive.

External aid: The LTTE's overt organizations support Tamil separatism by lobbying foreign governments and the United Nations. The LTTE also uses its international contacts to procure weapons, communications, and bomb-making equipment. The LTTE exploits large Tamil communities in North America, Europe, and Asia to obtain funds and supplies for its fighters in Sri Lanka. Information obtained since the mid-1980s indicates that some Tamil communities in Europe are also involved in narcotics smuggling. Tamils historically have served as drug couriers moving narcotics into Europe.

LOYALIST VOLUNTEER FORCE

Description: Terrorist group formed in late 1996 as a faction of Ulster Volunteer Force, but received no publicity until early 1997. The group is composed mainly of hard-liners from the UVF who are opposed to the peace process. Decommissioned some of its weapons in 1998.

Activities: Using Powergel explosives, typical of the many loyalist groups, they undertook bombings, kidnapings, and shooting attacks.

Strength: 150 or so members.

Location/Area of operation: Northern Ireland, Ireland.

External Aid: None.

MANUEL RODRIGUEZ PATRIOTIC FRONT (FPMR)

Description: Founded in 1983, the FPMR was originally the armed wing of the Chilean Communist Party and was named for the hero of Chile's war of independence against Spain. The group splintered into two factions in the late 1980s, and one faction became a political party in 1991. The dissident wing FPMR/D is Chile's only remaining active terrorist group.

Activities: FPMR/D attacks civilians and international targets, including U.S. businesses and Mormon churches in Chile. In 1993 FPMR/D bombed two McDonald's restaurants and attempted to bomb a Kentucky Fried Chicken. Successful Chilean government counterterrorist operations have significantly undercut the organization. The FPMR staged an escape from prison using a helicopter in December 1996.

Strength: Now believed to have between 50 and 100 members.

Location/Area of operation: Chile.

External aid: None.

MORANZANIST PATRIOTIC FRONT (FPM)

Description: A radical, leftist Honduran terrorist group that first appeared in the late 1980s.

Activities: Attacks on U.S., mainly military, personnel in Honduras. Claimed responsibility for attack on a bus in March 1990 that wounded seven U.S. servicemen. Claimed bombing of Peace Corps office in December 1988; a bus bombing that wounded three U.S. servicemen in February 1989, an attack on a U.S. convoy in April 1989, and a grenade attack that wounded seven U.S. soldiers in La Ceiba in July 1989. These are said to be in protest of U.S. intervention in Honduran affairs.

Strength: Unknown, probably relatively small.

Location/Area of operation: Honduras.

External aid: Had ties to the former government of Nicaragua and possibly Cuba.

MUJAHEDIN-E KHALQ ORGANIZATION (MEK OR MKO)

aka: The National Liberation Army of Iran (NLA, the militant wing of the MEK), the People's Mujahedin of Iran (PMOI), National Council of Resistance (NCR), Muslim Iranian Student's Society (front organization used to garner financial support)

Description: Formed in the 1960s by the college-educated children of Iranian merchants, the MEK sought to counter what was perceived as excessive Western influence in the Shah's regime. In the 1970s, the MEK concluded that violence was the only way to bring about change in Iran. Since then, the MEK, following a philosophy that mixes Marxism and Islam, has developed into the largest and most-active armed Iranian dissident group. Its history is studded with anti-Western activity and most recently, attacks on the interests of the clerical regime in Iran and abroad.

Activities: The MEK directs a worldwide campaign against the Iranian government that stresses propaganda and occasionally uses terrorist violence. During the 1970s, the MEK staged terrorist attacks inside Iran to destabilize and embarrass the Shah's regime. The group killed several U.S. military personnel and civilians working on defense projects in Tehran. The group also supported the takeover in 1979 of the U.S. Embassy in Tehran. In April 1992, the MEK carried out attacks on Iranian embassies in thirteen different countries, demonstrating the group's ability to mount large-scale operations overseas.

The normal pace of operations increased during the "Operation Great Brahman" in February 2000, when the group claimed it launched a dozen attacks against Iran.

Strength: Several thousand fighters based in Iraq with an extensive overseas support structure. Most of the fighters are organized in the MEK's National Liberation Army (NLA).

Location/Area of operation: In the 1980s, the MEK leaders were forced by Iranian security forces to flee to France. Most resettled in Iraq by 1987. Since the mid-1980s, the MEK has not mounted terrorist operations in Iran at a level similar to its activities in the 1970s. Aside from the National Liberation Army's attacks into Iran toward the end of the Iran-Iraq war and occasional NLA cross border incursions since, the MEK's attacks on Iran have mounted to little more than harassment. The MEK has had more success in confronting Iranian representatives overseas through propaganda and street demonstrations.

External aid: Beyond support from Iraq, the MEK uses front organizations to solicit contributions from expatriate Iranian communities.

MRTA
(see Tupac Amaru Revolutionary Movement)

NATIONAL LIBERATION ARMY (ELN)
Colombia, includes Nestor Paz Zamora Commission (CNPZ)
Description: ELN claims to be a resuscitation of the group established by

Che Guevara in the 1960s. Includes numerous small factions of indigenous subversive groups, including CNPZ, which is largely inactive today.

Activities: ELN and CNPZ have attacked U.S. interests in the past, but more recently have focused almost exclusively on Colombian domestic targets. Attacks on the energy infrastructure inflicted major damage to pipelines and electric-distribution systems.

Strength: Approximately 3,000 to 6,000 armed combatants and unknown number of active supporters.

Location/Area of operation: Mostly in rural and mountainous areas of north, northeast, and southwest Colombia and Venezuela border regions.

External aid: Cuba provides some medical care and political consultation.

NEW PEOPLE'S ARMY (NPA)

Description: The guerrilla arm of the Communist Party of the Philippines (CPP), an avowedly Maoist group formed in December 1969 with the aim of overthrowing the government through protracted guerrilla warfare. Although primarily a rural-based guerrilla group, the NPA has an active urban infrastructure to carry out terrorism. Uses city-based assassination squads called "sparrow units." Derives most of its funding from contributions of supporters and so-called revolutionary taxes extorted from local business.

Activities: NPA is in disarray because of a split in the CPP, a lack of money, and successful government operations. With the U.S. military gone from the country, NPA has engaged in urban terrorism against the police, corrupt politicians, and drug traffickers.

Strength: Estimated between 6,000 and 8,000.

Location/Area of operation: Operates in rural Luzon, Visayas, and parts of Mindanao. Has cells in Manila and other metropolitan centers.

External aid: Unknown.

APPENDIX

ORANGE VOLUNTEERS (OV)

Description: Extremist Protestant terrorist group comprised largely of disgruntled loyalist hard-liners who split from groups observing the cease-fire. OV seeks to prevent a political settlement with Irish nationalists by attacking Catholic interests in Northern Ireland.

Activities: The OV declared a cease-fire in September 2000, but the group maintains ability to conduct bombings, arson, beatings, and possibly robberies.

Strength: Up to 20 hard-core members, some of whom are experienced in terrorist tactics and bomb making.

Location/Area of operation: Northern Ireland.

External Aid: None.

THE PALESTINE ISLAMIC JIHAD (PIJ)

Description: The PIJ, which originated among militant Palestinians in the Gaza strip during the 1970s, is a series of loosely affiliated factions rather than a cohesive group. The PIJ is committed to the creation of an Islamic Palestinian state and the destruction of Israel through holy war. Because of its strong support for Israel, the United States has been identified as an enemy of the PIJ. The PIJ also opposes moderate Arab governments that it believes have been tainted by Western secularism.

Activities: PIJ militants have threatened to retaliate against Israel and the United States for the murder of PIJ leader Fathi Shaqaqi in Malta in October 1995. It has carried out suicide-bombing attacks against Israeli targets in the West Bank, Gaza strip, and Israel. The PIJ has threatened to attack U.S. interests in Jordan. Conducted at least three attacks against Israeli interests in late 2000.

Strength: Unknown.

Location/Area of operation: Primarily Israel and the occupied territories and other parts of the Middle East, including Jordan and Lebanon. The largest faction is based in Syria.

External aid: Probably receives financial assistance from Iran and possibly some logistic assistance from Syria.

PALESTINE LIBERATION FRONT (PLF)

Description: Terrorist group that broke away from the PFLP-GC in mid-1970s. Later split again into pro-PLO, pro-Syrian, and pro-Libyan factions. Pro-PLO faction led by Muhammad Abbas (Abu Abbas), who became a member of the PLO Executive Committee in 1984, but left it in 1991.

Activities: The Abu Abbas-led faction has carried out attacks against Israel. Abbas' group was also responsible for the attack in 1985 on the cruise ship, *Achille Lauro*, and the murder of U.S. citizen Leon Klinghoffer. A warrant for Abu Abbas' arrest is still outstanding in Italy.

Strength: Unknown.

Location/Area of operation: PLO faction was based in Tunisia until the *Achille Lauro* attack, now based in Iraq.

External aid: Receives logistic and military support mainly from PLO, but also from Libya and Iraq.

PARTY OF DEMOCRATIC KAMPUCHEA (KHMER ROUGE)

Description: Communist insurgency that is trying to destabilize the Cambodian government. Under Pol Pot's leadership, the Khmer Rouge conducted a campaign of genocide in which more than one million people were killed during its four years in power in the late 1970s. Although there were large-scale defections from the Khmer Rouge to Cambodian government forces in 1996, the group may still be considered dangerous.

Activities: The Khmer Rouge is now engaged in a low-level insurgency against the Cambodian government. Although its victims are mainly Cambodian villagers, the Khmer Rouge has occasionally kidnaped and killed foreigners traveling in remote rural areas.

Pol Pot was "tried" by his own comrades in late July 1997. What this will mean to the people living in the land-mine-strewn and malaria-ridden areas of Cambodia is unclear at this time.

Strength: 1,000 to 2,000.

Location/Area of operation: Operates in outlying provinces in Cambodia, particularly in pockets along the Thailand border.

External aid: None.

PKK
(see Kurdistan Workers' Party)

POPULAR FRONT FOR THE LIBERATION OF PALESTINE (PFLP)

Description: Marxist-Leninist group founded in 1967 by George Habash as a member of the PLO. Advocates a Pan-Arab revolution. Opposes the Declaration of Principles signed in 1993 and has suspended participation in the PLO.

Activities: Committed numerous international terrorist attacks during the 1970s. Since 1978, PFLP has carried out numerous attacks against Israeli or moderate Arab targets, including the killing of a settler and her son in December 1996.

Strength: Some 800.

Location/Area of operation: Syria, Lebanon, Israel and the occupied territories.

External aid: Receives most of its financial and military assistance from Syria and Libya.

POPULAR FRONT FOR THE LIBERATION OF PALESTINE- GENERAL COMMAND (PFLP-GC)

Description: Split from the PFLP in 1968, claiming that it wanted to focus more on fighting and less on politics. Violently opposed to Arafat's PLO. Led by Ahmad Jibril, a former captain in the Syrian army. Closely allied with, supported by, and probably directed by Syria.

Activities: Has carried out numerous cross-border terrorist attacks into Israel using unusual means, such as hot-air balloons and motorized hang gliders.

Strength: Several hundred.

Location/Area of operation: Headquartered in Damascus, bases in Lebanon, and cells in Europe.

External aid: Received logistic and military support from Syria, its chief sponsor, financial support from Libya, safe haven in Syria. Also receives support from Iran.

PROVISIONAL IRISH REPUBLICAN ARMY
(see Irish Republican Army)

AL-QAEDA
(proper name is al-Qa'ida)

Description: Established by Osama bin Laden in the late 1980s to bring together Arabs who fought in Afghanistan against the Soviet invasion. Helped to finance, recruit, transport, and train Sunni Muslim extremists for the Afghan resistance. Current goal is to establish a pan-Islamic caliphate throughout the world by working with allied Islamic extremist groups. The goal is to overthrow regimes it deems "non-Islamic" and expelling Westerners and non-Muslims from Muslim countries. Issued statement under banner of "the World Islamic Front for Jihad Against Jews and Crusaders" in February 1998, stating that it was the duty of all Muslims to kill U.S. citizens, civilian and military, and their allies everywhere.

Activities: Plotted to carry out terrorist operations against U.S. and Israeli tourists visiting Jordan for the millennial celebrations. (Jordanian authorities thwarted the planned attacks and put twenty-eight suspects on trial.) Conducted the bombings in August 1998 of the U.S. embassies in Nairobi, Kenya, and Dar es Salaam, Tanzania, that killed 301 people and injured more than 5,000 others. Claims to have shot down U.S. helicopters and killed U.S. servicemen in Somalia in 1993 and to have conducted three bombings that targeted U.S. troops in Aden, Yemen, in December 1992. On September 11, 2001, using four hijacked airliners, destroyed both towers of the World Trade Center and inflicted massive damage on the Pentagon. Continues to train, finance, and provide logistic support to terrorist groups in support of these goals. With the Taliban defeated, al-Qaeda came under intense attack, and its cave complexes in the White Mountains, close to the Pakistan border, were captured by Northern Alliance troops.

Strength: May have several hundred to several thousand members. Also serves as a focal point or umbrella organization for a worldwide network that includes many Sunni Islamic extremist groups such as Egyptian Islamic Jihad, some members of al-Gama'at al-Islamiyya, the Islamic Movement of Uzbekistan and the Harakat ul-Mujahidin. After the capture of Tora Bora, the remaining members fled to Pakistan and other Muslim countries.

Location/area of operation: al-Qaeda has a worldwide reach, has cells in a number of countries and is reinforced by its ties to Sunni extremist networks.

External aid: Bin Laden, a member of a billionaire Saudi family, is said to have inherited approximately $300 million that he uses to finance the group. Al-Qaeda also maintains moneymaking front organizations, solicits donations from like-minded supporters, and illicitly siphons funds from donations to Muslim charitable organizations. The organization also earns money from the Taliban heroin trade.

REAL IRA (RIRA)
aka: True IRA

Description: Formed in 1998 as clandestine armed wing of the 32-County Sovereignty Movement, a "political pressure group" dedicated to removing British forces from Northern Ireland and unifying Ireland.

Activities: Bombings, assassinations, and robberies. Has attempted several unsuccessful bomb attacks on the UK mainland. Claimed responsibility for the Omagh, Northern Ireland, bombing in August 1998 that killed 29 and injured 220 people. Recently appears to observe the cease-fire.

Strength: About 70 and possibly other sympathizers.

Location/Area of operation: Northern Ireland, Irish Republic, and Great Britain.

External aid: Funds from U.S. sympathizers, weapons from the Balkans.

RED HAND DEFENDERS (RHD)

Description: Extremist terrorist group composed largely of Protestant hard-liners from loyalist groups observing the cease-fire.

Activities: RHD has carried out numerous pipe-bombing and arson attacks against "soft" civilian targets such as homes, churches, and private businesses to cause outrage in the Republican community.

Strength: Up to 20 members, many with experience in terrorist tactics and bomb making.

Location/Area of operation: Northern Ireland.

External Aid: None.

REVOLUTIONARY ARMED FORCES OF COLOMBIA (FARC)

Description: The largest, best-trained, best-equipped, and most-capable guerrilla organization in Colombia. Established in 1966 as a military wing of the Colombian Communist Party. Goal is to overthrow the government and ruling class. Organized along military lines, includes at least one urban front. Has been anti-U.S. since its inception. Led by Manuel Marulanda.

Activities: Armed attacks against Colombian political and military targets. Many members pursue criminal activities, carrying out kidnapings for profit and bank robberies. Foreign citizens often are targets of FARC kidnaping. The group traffics in drugs and has well-documented ties to narco-traffickers mainly through providing armed protection.

Strength: Approximately 9,000 to 12,000 armed combatants and an unknown number of supporters, mostly in rural areas.

Location/Area of operation: Colombia, with occasional operations in Venezuela, Panama, and Ecuador.

External aid: Cuba provides some medical aid.

REVOLUTIONARY ORGANIZATION 17 NOVEMBER (17 NOVEMBER)

Description: A radical leftist group established in 1975 and named for the November 1973 student uprising in Greece protesting the military regime. The group is anti-Greek establishment, anti-U.S., anti-Turkey, anti-NATO. Committed to the ouster of U.S. bases, removal of Turkish military presence from Cyprus, and severing of Greece's ties with NATO and the

European Union (EU). Organization is obscure, possibly affiliated with other Greek terrorist groups.

Activities: Initial attacks were assassinations of senior U.S. officials and Greek public figures. Added bombings in 1980s. Since 1990, has expanded targets to include EU facilities and foreign firms investing in Greece and has added improvised rocket attacks to its methods. Most recent attack was the murder in June 2000 of British defense attaché Stephen Saunders.

Strength: Unknown, but presumed to be small.

Location/Area of operation: Athens, Greece.

External aid: Unknown.

REVOLUTIONARY PEOPLE'S LIBERATION PARTY/FRONT (DHKP/C)
aka: Devrimci Sol (Revolutionary Left), Dev Sol.

Description: Originally formed in 1978 as Devrimci Sol, or Dev Sol, it was a splinter faction of the Turkish People's Liberation Party/Front. Renamed in 1994 after factional infighting, it still espouses a Marxist ideology and is virulently anti-U.S. and anti-NATO. The group finances its activities chiefly through armed robberies and extortion.

Activities: Since the late 1980s has concentrated attacks against current and retired Turkish security and military officials. Began a new campaign against foreign interests in 1990. Protesting the Gulf War, it assassinated two U.S. military contractors and wounded an American air force officer. Launched rockets at U.S. Consulate in Istanbul in 1992. Assassinated a prominent Turkish businessman in early 1996, its first significant act as DHKP/C. A series of safe-house raids and arrests by Turkish police in the past three years weakened the group significantly. Turkish security forces stormed prison wards controlled by the DHKP/C in December 2000, transferring militants to cell-type penitentiaries.

Strength: Unknown.

Location/Area of operation: Carries out attacks in Turkey, primarily in Istanbul, Ankara, Izmir, and Adana. Conducts fund-raising operations in Europe.

External aid: Possible training support from radical Palestinians.

REVOLUTIONARY PEOPLE'S STRUGGLE (ELA)

Description: An extreme leftist group that developed out of the opposition to the military junta that ruled Greece from 1967 to 1974. Formed in 1971, the ELA is a self-described revolutionary, anticapitalist, and antiimperialist group, which has declared its opposition to "imperialist domination, exploitation, and oppression." The ELA is strongly anti-U.S. and seeks the removal of U.S. military forces from Greece.

Activities: Since 1974 the group has carried out bombings against Greek government and economic targets as well as U.S. military and business facilities. In 1986 the group stepped up attacks on Greek government and commercial interests. In November 1990, a raid on a safe house revealed a weapons cache and direct contacts with other Greek terrorist groups, including 1 May and Revolutionary Solidarity (these smaller groups are not described). During 1991 ELA and 1 May claimed joint responsibility for more than 20 bombings. Greek police believe they have established a link between the ELA and the Revolutionary Organization 17 November.

Strength: Unknown.

Location/Area of operation: Greece.

External aid: Received aid in the 1980s from Carlos. No known foreign sponsors.

REVOLUTIONARY UNITED FRONT (RUF)

Description: The RUF is a loosely organized group, but an effective guerrilla force because of its flexibility and brutal discipline. They are seeking to overthrow the government of Sierra Leone and retain control of the lucrative diamond-producing regions of the country. Funding is mainly through sale of diamonds produced in its areas of control.

Activities: The RUF uses guerrilla, criminal, and other terror tactics to fight the government, intimidate civilians, and keep peacekeeping units in check. In 2000 it held hundreds of UN peacekeepers hostage until their release was negotiated. The RUF's chief sponsor is said to be Liberian President Charles Taylor.

Strength: Estimated at several thousand fighters and probably an equal number of sympathizers.

Location/Area of operation: Sierra Leone, Liberia, Guinea.

External Aid: Liberia.

SENDERO LUMINOSO (SHINING PATH, SL)

Description: Larger of Peru's two insurgencies, SL is among the world's most-ruthless guerrilla organizations. Formed in the late 1960s by then-university professor Abimael Guzman. Stated goal is to destroy existing Peruvian institutions and replace them with a peasant revolutionary regime. Also wants to rid Peru of foreign influences. Guzman's capture in September 1992 was a major blow, as were arrests of other SL leaders in 1995, defections among members, and President Alberto Fujimori's amnesty program for repentant terrorists.

Activities: Engages in particularly brutal forms of terrorism, including the indiscriminate use of bombs. Almost every institution in Peru has been a target of SL violence. Has bombed diplomatic missions of several countries in Peru, including the U.S. Embassy. Carries out bombing campaigns and selective assassinations. Has attacked U.S. businesses since its inception. Involved in cocaine trade.

Strength: Approximately 100 to 200 armed militants, larger number of supporters, mostly in rural areas. Its strength has been vastly reduced by arrests and desertions.

Location/Area of operation: Peru. Rural-based, with some terrorist attacks in the capital.

External aid: None.

SIKH TERRORISM

Description: Sikh terrorism is sponsored by expatriate and Indian Sikh groups who want to carve out an independent Sikh state called Khalistan (Land of the Pure) from Indian territory. Active groups include Babbar Khalsa, Azad Khalistan Babbar Khalse Force, Khalistan Liberation Front, and Khalistan Commando Force. Many of these groups operate under umbrella organizations, the most significant of which is the Second Panthis Committee.

Activities: Sikh attacks in India are mounted against Indian officials and facilities, other Sikhs, and Hindus. They include assassinations, bombings, and kidnapings. These attacks have dropped markedly since 1992 as Indian security forces have killed or captured many senior Sikh militant leaders. Total civilian deaths in Punjab have declined more than 95 percent since more than 3,300 civilians died in 1991. The drop results largely from Indian army, paramilitary, and police successes against extremist groups.
Strength: Unknown.

Location/Area of operation: Northern India, Western Europe, Southeast Asia, and North America.

External aid: Sikh militant cells are active internationally, and extremists gather funds from overseas Sikh communities. Sikh expatriates have formed a variety of international organizations that lobby for the Sikh cause overseas. Most prominent are the World Sikh Organization and the International Sikh Youth Federation.

TUPAC AMARU REVOLUTIONARY MOVEMENT (MRTA)

Description: Traditional Marxist-Leninist revolutionary movement formed in 1983. Objective remains to rid Peru of imperialism and establish a Marxist regime. The movement has suffered from defections and government counterterrorist successes in addition to infighting and loss of leftist support.

Activities: Bombings, kidnapings, ambushes, assassinations. Previously responsible for a large number of anti-U.S. attacks. Activity dropped off dramatically until the December 1996 attack on the Japanese ambassador's residence. More than four hundred hostages were taken by twenty-three MRTA members during a diplomatic reception. The last eighty-three hostages were released in April 1997 when Peruvian security forces stormed the residence and killed all MRTA hostage takers. Today most members of the MRTA are in jail.

Strength: Unknown, believed to be no more than 100.

Location/Area of operation: Peru.

External aid: None.

APPENDIX

UNITED SELF-DEFENSE FORCES/GROUP
OF COLOMBIA (AUC)

Description: Commonly called paramilitaries or autodefensas, AUC is an umbrella organization formed in 1997 to consolidate local and regional groups. The AUC is supported by the economic elites, drug traffickers, and local communities lacking effective government security.

Activities: The Colombian National Police reported 804 assassinations, 203 kidnapings, and 75 massacres during 2000 attributed to the AUC.

Strength: In early 2001, the government estimated that there were 8,000 paramilitary fighters, including former military and insurgent personnel.

Location/Area of operation: The main strong points are in the north and northwest.

External Aid: None.

• • •

An interagency study commissioned by former Attorney General Janet Reno concluded that the U.S. lacks ability to combat extremist attacks. The report states: "Increased activity by small cells of terrorists or individuals who are inspired by, but not affiliated with, terrorist groups, thus making them harder to identify and stop." The study further states that failure of various government agencies to share information, especially on potential domestic perpetrators, undermines the effort to combat terrorism.

Why the above list of unsavory characters? Because they are increasingly targeting the United States and her citizens, and to combat these groups, our government is trampling over the rights of all Americans. We are planning to introduce national identity cards, limit access to public offices, and as such, limit American freedoms. The study referred to above called for federal and state agencies to share information to catch the new breed of terrorist. The new breed is identified as lone extremists inspired by acts of terrorist groups.

A broad definition would target all those of who follow Islam, are of Middle Eastern descent, former members of the armed forces, people questioning the slow encroachment of regulators over personal freedoms until we have a 100 million potential terrorists. What a wonderful way to enlarge police and intelligence agencies budgets at the expense of social spending.

PROFILES OF TERRORIST ORGANIZATIONS

Could terrorists hijack a nuclear device? Consider that a disgruntled former Russian military officer offered Greenpeace a nuclear warhead. One member of the Aum Shinrikyo sect worked at Russia's Kurchatov nuclear physics institute. Either of these could pose a threat to world stability. The terrorists motto seems to be "the more bizarre the act of terror, the better." What could be better than getting their hands on a nuclear device from either one of the nuclear powers?

SUMMARY

Terrorists have new tools in their arsenal. These range from chemicals, biologicals on through cyberspace. For example, you can scrape off anthrax microbes from the flesh of diseased animals. Where an anthrax-infected animal dies, the ground will crawl with anthrax microbes for decades. Once cultured, this deadly cargo can be transported in a test tube, which won't set off the metal detectors at airports or in buildings, or sent through the U.S. mail. The poison ricin can be extracted from the castor-bean plant and smeared over objects. It's a simple method of killing. All the victim has to do is touch the smeared object.

In information warfare, the heart of the system can be infiltrated, and using today's computer tools, havoc wreaked on the country. Imagine the president's image appearing on your TV telling you to evacuate all major cities because of nuclear terrorists and to disregard any following messages because the television networks are vulnerable to disinformation. Then in a few minutes, the president is on TV again telling you to disregard the previous message. With the use of computer graphics, stored video images, and other tools, this can be done. We have time to prepare for these incidents now.

The number of international terrorist incidents had fallen, from a peak of 665 in 1987, to 304 in 1997, a twenty-five-year low. About two-thirds of these attacks were minor acts of politically motivated violence against commercial targets, the deadliest attack occurred in Egypt on November 17, 1997, when members of the Al-Gama'at al-Islamiyya fundamentalist group shot and killed fifty-eight foreign tourists and four Egyptian nationals in the Valley of Kings near Luxor. While the incidence of international terrorism dropped sharply in the last decade, the overall threat of terrorism remains very serious.

This was evidenced on September 11, 2001, with a death toll of some three thousand. Now we see a trend continuing toward more ruthless attacks on mass civilian targets and the use of more powerful bombs. The threat of terrorists using materials of mass destruction is an issue of growing concern. We saw the start of it through the anthrax-laced mail.

Terrorism by religious fanatics and groups manipulating religion, especially Islam, for political purposes continued to dominate international terrorism. Organized groups such as HAMAS and the Palestine Islamic Jihad, which were behind the bus bombings in Tel Aviv and Jerusalem, and the al-Gama'at al-Islamiyya, which continued acts of terror in Egypt, remain active and dangerous. Freelance, transnational terrorists, many of whom were trained in Afghanistan and were backed by international terrorist financiers such as the Saudi dissident Osama bin Laden, are a growing factor. Ethnic terrorism in such places as Chechnya, Tajikistan, and Sri Lanka took a heavy toll, and the Kurdistan Workers' Party maintains its campaign of terror against Turkey.

The counterterrorist policy of the United States stresses three general rules:

- First, make no deals with terrorists, and do not submit to blackmail.

- Second, treat terrorists as criminals, pursue them aggressively, and apply the rule of law.

- Third, apply maximum pressure on states that sponsor and support terrorists by imposing economic, diplomatic, and political sanctions and by urging other states to do likewise.

Terrorism springs from one common fountain: rage. And rage can be traced to one common cause: pain. Jacques Ellul explains this in his book,

SUMMARY

Anatomy of Revolution, but tragically most people today refuse to understand terrorism. Tragic is the appropriate word for this situation because the public's refusal to dig down to the roots will inevitably lead to more terrorism and deaths, both domestic and international, in spite of the statistics. Today's terrorists may become tomorrow's statesmen as shown throughout history.

Today few people deny that domestic and international terrorism is likely to increase during the foreseeable future. We are relying on police and military protective measures, which instead of reducing the impulses behind terrorism will increase the level of terrorism. Why is that? Because we are not getting at the basic causes of terrorism, we are only treating its symptoms. Do not take this for condoning terrorist acts. This would be like blaming the victims for their misfortune.

The unfortunate tendency to centralize public-safety functions results in extended response times to incidents and creates another inviting target.

A permanent war footing both at home and abroad is hardly the responsible answer. So we have opted for the panacea of police power, and this is supported by the majority. The unfortunate tendency to centralize public-safety functions results in extended response times to incidents and creates another inviting target. Even though most politicians know that we are doing nothing to dig out terrorism by its roots, they rely on increased police powers to combat terrorism because seemingly something is being done. This kind of response actually creates domestic terror by creating cynicism, one of the primary emotions leading to the pain and rage that lie beneath all acts of terrorism.

The deadly cycle of counterproductive government action leads to frustration, frustration yields to cynicism, cynicism leads to hopelessness, hopelessness leads to pain, pain leads to rage, and rage leads to bombs—ever-bigger bombs—until the Million Man March or something like it is incinerated with a megaton sleeper nuclear device irradiating inside the Beltway. At that point, terrorism becomes a driving force in the world around us. We all become slaves to the need to combat terror.

Given our understanding that terrorism is going to increase, and since we have some real insight into the dynamics behind terrorism, isn't it possible that we can do what is necessary to defuse the march toward greater terrorism? Certainly it is possible, but to do so we need a strategy that can stop the pain at the root of terrorism. Such a strategy begins by identifying the cause of the pain. If your finger hurts and you notice a splinter embedded in your skin, you know by removing the splinter, the pain is likely to be removed with it. Maybe not immediately, but the pain will go away.

Is there a splinter in the body politic of the United States of America? Actually, this nation suffers from a malady much-more dangerous and grave than a splinter. We are suffering from a disease called amnesia of American history. Amnesia is a dangerous ailment for any nation, but for one like the U.S., it can be fatal. We are trying to control more and more minute aspects of American life. To do so in a nation founded upon tolerance goes against all the principles of the founders of the union. The settlers of this land came here to escape tyranny, find religious freedom, and have a say in the running of their country.

At one time, we knew who the terrorists were: a handful of Middle Eastern or leftist political movements, sponsored and protected by governments, bent on achieving their well-advertised ideological goals through death and intimidation. The next generation of terrorists is more obscure, an assemblage of disparate fanatics pursuing unique or mysterious agendas, with only the capacity for random violence in common. The experts feel that the rise of apocalyptic sects and Islamic extremism has merged with the easy availability of chemical and biological weapons that can kill thousands in one attack. The potential for random murder and catastrophic governmental disruption lies within reach of small, unsophisticated, and irresponsible groups of true believers.

Even though radical groups have long had the power to kill more people than they actually have, the fact that they held back somewhat suggests they imposed certain restraints on themselves. Most such groups viewed themselves as political activists rather than wanton killers. They had to appeal to potential supporters of their program and were wary of producing a backlash of revulsion by using the most-repellent methods. The Cold War and the rules of state-sponsored terrorism curtailed their freedom of action.

Governments knew more or less who was sponsoring whom, and the threat of retaliation was always present, as demonstrated when the Reagan administration sent U.S. bombers to hit Libya in 1986 in retaliation for its support of several terrorist acts. As a pundit said, "President Reagan settled out of court." The end of the Cold War and the beginnings of the Middle East peace process have taken Eastern European and some Muslim governments out of the sponsorship business.

At the same time, however, the collapse of the Soviet empire, the creation of new states, and the breakup of others have triggered an explosion of ethnic conflicts, with racial and religious hatreds mixed in, giving fresh scope to terrorist freelancers. Much of the violence committed today in the name of Islam is the work of small, loosely organized cells that emerge for little more than a single act of random vengeance. Sections of Pakistan are ungovernable safe havens for the remnants of twenty thousand zealot volunteers from Muslim countries all over the world who joined the Afghan mujahedin in their holy war against the Soviets. An estimated one thousand fundamentalist fighters still gather in the country's lawless reaches to train, fight, and egg each other on.

Some freelance terrorists have taken up residence in the U.S. They have brought with them a brand of activism previously unknown except for occasional episodes of violence against each other, as when Sikh extremists attacked officials of the Indian government in U.S. cities. Most of these terrorists are religious fanatics, and whenever religion is involved, more people are killed.

Then we have the emergence of megaterrorism. Examples abound. In March 1993, thirteen car bombs exploded simultaneously in the financial district of Bombay, resulting in more than three hundred killed and one thousand wounded. The 1993 World Trade Center explosion was designed to topple one tower into the other. However, it was not until September 11, 2001, that this was achieved. The loss of life and property was great enough to move the U.S. to war footing.

The activities of Chechen guerrillas in taking entire villages hostage and the hijacking of a Turkish ferry on the Black Sea all demonstrate the length to which certain groups are willing to go to achieve their ends. All of these are in part a response to the behavior of the opposition. Russian carpet bombing of Chechen towns and villages, which may have killed more than thirty thousand people, forces us to ask ourselves, who are the megaterrorists, the Russians or the Chechens? The Chechens view this as warfare.

Russia, the onetime exporter and financier of terrorist movements worldwide, is now experiencing terrorism inside her borders. The Russians are not making much headway in solving many highly visible terrorist acts, including a series of bombs placed in public transportation vehicles in Moscow and elsewhere in the country, and a bombing that leveled a nine-story apartment building in Kaspiysk, killing more than fifty. Then there are the acts of Chechen rebels, as mentioned above.

"Cyberterror" may be a new weapon to join the arsenal of terrorists worldwide. Michael Vlahos argues that there is a parallel between cyberterrorists and the James Gang, a noted band of criminals who terrorized

SUMMARY

the American West in the late 1860s by both riding and raiding trains. He points out that the James Gang took advantage of the widespread and rapid introduction of a new technology—railroads—by using trains to carry them to and from their targets (other trains).

The gang was very successful with this entirely new type of crime for some time until law enforcement agencies, and eventually society itself, adapted to the new conditions. Similarly, Vlahos suggests, the Internet will become both the target and the instrument of cyberterrorists. In cyberspace, a new frontier and a savage, primitive medium capable of wrecking economies of people and whole groups, technological developments far outpace essential controls.

As a result, Vlahos says society will be most vulnerable in the present transition period. In fact, he adds, our vulnerability to megaterrorism in cyberspace may even lead to the introduction of authoritarian controls to protect against such attacks. But in Vlahos' view, the development of a civic culture of responsibility in cyberspace could be far-more effective in the long run. It was, after all, the citizens of Northfield, Minnesota, who put an end to the James Gang.

Borders mean little to these organizations. Religious fanaticism plays a greater role in their activities than ever. This is why religious cults are monitored more than ever by police and intelligence organizations.

Terrorism is part of the new millennium. Terrorists are lurking in our neighborhoods. But by being prepared, you can survive.